中国文化概况

An Overview of Chinese Culture

(Chinese-English Bilingual)

汉英双语

微课版

主编 熊英
副主编 鞠玮玉 李若水
编者 谢明明 高娜娜 杨菁

大连理工大学出版社

图书在版编目(CIP)数据

中国文化概况：汉、英 / 熊英主编. -- 大连：大连理工大学出版社，2023.1（2024.2重印）
ISBN 978-7-5685-3241-9

Ⅰ. ①中… Ⅱ. ①熊… Ⅲ. ①中华文化—概况—汉、英 Ⅳ. ①K203

中国版本图书馆CIP数据核字(2021)第217352号

大连理工大学出版社出版

地址：大连市软件园路80号　　　邮政编码：116023
发行：0411-84708842　邮购：0411-84706041　传真：0411-84701466
E-mail：dutp@dutp.cn　　　URL：https://www.dutp.cn
大连日升彩色印刷有限公司印刷　　大连理工大学出版社发行

幅面尺寸：185mm×260mm	印张：9.25	字数：214千字
2023年1月第1版		2024年2月第2次印刷
责任编辑：王赫男		责任校对：徐　丹
	封面设计：张　莹	

ISBN 978-7-5685-3241-9　　　　　　　　　　定价：45.00元

本书如有印装质量问题，请与我社发行部联系更换。

前 言

　　为帮助中国学生与英语学习者尽早融入跨文化语言学习氛围，方便广大来华留学生快速适应在中国学习和生活的环境，编者依据多年教学实践经验，组织团队编写了这本《中国文化概况（汉英双语）》。本教材涵盖中国历史与地理，文学与传统节日，书画与音乐，自然与人文景观，饮食文化、用餐礼仪与茶文化，传统服饰与艺术品，网络与现代生活，古代与现代教育和历史与现代国际交流九个章节，呈现了中国文化的丰富璀璨，架起了沟通中外的文化桥梁。课文内容图文并茂，课后练习设计有利于学生展开思考、讨论和拓展学习，在引导学生了解中国文化的同时，增强其跨文化交际能力，批判性思维能力以及语言的综合运用能力。

　　本教材主要特色如下：

　　1. 充分体现"立德树人、教书育人"的理念，探索课程思政在"中国文化概况"课程中的全面应用。通过"文化对比""开放性研讨"等批判性思维教学和"好书推介"等引导式教学，充分展示真实、立体的中国文化，实现弘扬中国优秀传统文化，推介新时代中国精神，厚植"人类命运共同体"理念，加强"一带一路"倡议认同的教学目的。

　　2. 充分发挥纸质教材和数字化资源相融合的优势。作为"互联网+"的新形态教材，本书配有内容丰富的数字化教学资源。教材编写团队针对每章重、难点专门策划并组织录制了《中国文化概况（汉英双语）》配套系列微课，并创建线上教学平台（http://lxsxxyd.wxit.edu.cn/）。使用该教材的高校可共享教材配套的数字化教学资源，如：微课、PPT教学课件、电子教案等，亦可参与共建线上教学资源库。

　　3. 内容丰富、时效性强、适用性广。本教材既可用于高等院校有对外交流需求的学生学习使用，也可作为来华留学生"中国文化概况"必修课的教材。本教材正式出版之前，已在无锡职业技术学院马来西亚汉语中心、印尼汉语中心以讲义的形式进行了多轮试用，教学效果显著。

本教材由无锡职业技术学院熊英担任主编，鞠玮玉、李若水担任副主编，谢明明、高娜娜、杨菁担任编者。"泰国泰中罗勇工业园""江苏德龙镍业有限公司印尼分公司"等海外中资企业和"南非中国文化和国际教育交流中心孔子课堂"等在本教材的编写过程中给予了宝贵的意见及建议，在此一并表示感谢。

本教材涉及课题包括："一带一路"视域下高职院校国际化创新路径探索（中国教育国际交流协会2021年度"一带一路"教育国际交流研究专项重点课题）（熊英）；中-南非高等职业教育机电类专业联合培养探索与实践（中国教育国际交流协会"未来非洲-中非职业教育合作计划"2021年研究课题）（熊英）；基于《国际中文教育中文水平等级标准》的留学生中文线上教学应用研究（中国教育国际交流协会职教分会2021年重点课题）（鞠玮玉）；"双高"背景下基于跨文化适应理论的来华留学生教育管理研究（2020年江苏省教育厅思政专项课题）（李若水）。

由于编纂工作浩繁，疏漏在所难免，欢迎广大读者不吝指正，以求共同进步。

编　者

2023年1月

所有意见和建议请发往:dutpwy@163.com

欢迎访问教材服务网站:https://www.dutp.cn/fle/

联系电话:0411-84707604　84706231

Contents

Chapter	Lesson	Page
Chapter One 第一章 **History and Geography** 历史与地理	**Lesson 1 An Overview of History** 第一课 历史概况	002
	Lesson 2 An Overview of Geography 第二课 地理概况	011
Chapter Two 第二章 **Literature and Traditional Festivals** 文学与传统节日	**Lesson 1 Literature Works** 第一课 文学作品	022
	Lesson 2 Traditional Festivals 第二课 传统节日	028
Chapter Three 第三章 **Calligraphy, Painting and Music** 书画与音乐	**Lesson 1 Calligraphy and Painting** 第一课 书画	038
	Lesson 2 Music 第二课 音乐	047
Chapter Four 第四章 **The Natural Landscapes and Humanity Landscapes** 自然与人文景观	**Lesson 1 Natural Landscapes** 第一课 自然景观	056
	Lesson 2 Humanity Landscapes 第二课 人文景观	063
Chapter Five 第五章 **Culinary Culture, Dining Etiquette & Tea Culture** 饮食文化、用餐礼仪与茶文化	**Lesson 1 Culinary Culture** 第一课 饮食文化	072
	Lesson 2 Dining Etiquette and Tea Culture 第二课 用餐礼仪与茶文化	080

Chapter	Lesson	Page
Chapter Six 第六章 Traditional Clothing and Art Crafts 传统服饰与艺术品	Lesson 1 Traditional Clothing 第一课 传统服饰	088
	Lesson 2 Art Crafts 第二课 艺术品	095
Chapter Seven 第七章 Network and Modern Life 网络与现代生活	Lesson 1 Modern Online Platforms 第一课 当代网络平台	104
	Lesson 2 Modern Lifestyles 第二课 现代生活方式	110
Chapter Eight 第八章 Ancient and Modern Education 古代与现代教育	Lesson 1 Ancient Education 第一课 古代教育	116
	Lesson 2 Contemporary Education 第二课 现代教育	123
Chapter Nine 第九章 Historical and Modern International Exchanges 历史与现代国际交流	Lesson 1 Historical Cultural Exchanges 第一课 历史文化交流	128
	Lesson 2 Modern Cultural Exchanges 第二课 现代文化交流	135

Chapter One

第一章

历史与地理 History and Geography

Introduction

The People's Republic of China, referred to as "China", was established on October 1, 1949. China is one of the countries with the longest history and the most populous developing country in the world. China has a vast territory and its land area ranks third in the world. Chinese culture is broad, profound, colorful, and occupies an important position in the world cultural system. China is the world's second largest economy and continues to be the world's largest contributor to economic growth. It is also one of the countries with the most development potential in the world. In this chapter, a basic overview of China's history and geography is introduced.

Learning Goals

1. to have an overall understanding of Chinese history
2. to be able to name the main historical events in different historical periods of China
3. to learn China's geographical location and administrative divisions
4. to understand the basic characteristics of China's topography, climate and resources

第一课 历史概况
Lesson 1 An Overview of History

China's long history can be traced back to the Yuanmou Man's period about 1.7 million years ago. The ancient history of China started from this period and ended before the Opium War in 1840, and went through primitive society, slave society and feudal society. The modern history of China is from the Opium War in 1840 to the eve of the founding of the People's Republic of China in 1949. It is the historical stage of China in a semi-colonial and semi-feudal society. China's contemporary history dates from the establishment of the People's Republic of China on October 1, 1949.

Ancient China

Ancient China was piled up by the rise and fall of dynasties. These dynasties had different durations, different territories, and different levels of economic and social development. Among them, two dynasties that were more prosperous and powerful — the Han Dynasty (including the Western Han Dynasty and the Eastern Han Dynasty) and the Tang Dynasty — had a huge influence on the formation and shaping of Chinese culture.

中国的悠久历史可以追溯到大约一百七十万年前的元谋人时期。中国古代史就是从这一时期开始,到1840年鸦片战争前结束,历经原始社会、奴隶社会和封建社会。中国近代史则为1840年鸦片战争到1949年中华人民共和国成立前夕,是中国处于半殖民地半封建社会的历史阶段。中国现代史则是从1949年10月1日中华人民共和国成立开始。

古代中国

古代中国由一个个朝代的兴起和覆灭堆砌而成。这些朝代历时有长有短,领土面积有大有小,经济和社会发展水平也各不相同。其中,较为繁荣强盛的两个朝代——汉朝(包括西汉和东汉)和唐朝——对中国文化的形成和塑造产生了巨大的影响。

The Han Dynasty

The Han Dynasty is divided into two periods: the Western Han Dynasty and the Eastern Han Dynasty. After the fall of the Qin Dynasty, Liu Bang established the Han Dynasty and made Chang'an (now Xi'an) the capital, which was called the Western Han Dynasty in history. During the period of Emperor Wen and Emperor Jing, the social economy was restored and developed through the implementation of the policy of rest and recuperation, and the situation of "Rule of Wen and Jing" appeared. When Emperor Wu of the Han Dynasty came to the throne, the Western Han Dynasty was strong and culturally prosperous. Emperor Wu of the Han Dynasty took a series of measures, including strengthening the centralization of power, fighting against the Xiongnu and paying supreme tribute to Confucianism, so the rule of the Western Han Dynasty reached its peak. Affected by this, the people in the Han Dynasty were called "Han people" by the surrounding ethnic groups, and gradually formed "Han group" and "Han culture".

In the late Western Han Dynasty, due to the sharp social contradictions, peasant wars broke out, and the Western Han Dynasty went to extinction. In 25 AD, Liu Xiu, a member of the Han clan, became emperor, and he adopted the Han national title, and made Luoyang the capital, which was called the Eastern Han Dynasty. In the early Eastern Han Dynasty, Emperor Guangwu of the Han Dynasty adjusted his ruling policy to bring about the prosperity of social economy, called the "Rule of Guangwu". At the end of the Eastern Han Dynasty, the powerful landlord forces developed, the Yellow Turban Rebellion broke out, and the Han Dynasty began to gradually perish.

汉朝

汉朝分为西汉和东汉两个时期。秦朝灭亡后，刘邦建立了汉朝，定都长安（今西安），史称西汉。汉文帝和汉景帝时期，通过推行休养生息政策，社会经济得到恢复和发展，出现了"文景之治"的局面。汉武帝即位时，西汉国力强盛，文化繁荣。汉武帝通过采取加强中央集权、抗击匈奴和独尊儒术等一系列措施，使西汉的统治进入了鼎盛时期。受此影响，汉朝境内的人被周边少数民族称为"汉人"，并逐渐形成了"汉族"和"汉文化"。

西汉后期，由于社会矛盾尖锐，农民战争爆发，西汉走向灭亡。公元25年，汉室宗亲刘秀称帝，沿用汉的国号，定都洛阳，史称东汉。东汉初期的汉光武帝通过调整统治政策，使社会经济出现了"光武中兴"的繁荣局面。东汉末年，豪强地主势力发展，爆发了黄巾起义，汉朝开始逐渐走向灭亡。

The Tang Dynasty

The Tang Dynasty was established in 618 AD by Li Yuan, a nobleman in the late Sui Dynasty, and its capital was Chang'an. Later, on the basis of Emperor Taizong's "Prosperity of Zhenguan" and the effective governance of Wu Zetian, the only empress in Chinese history, Emperor Xuanzong carried out reforms, and the country's strength reached its peak, which was called the "Heyday of Kaiyuan" in history. At this time, the Tang Dynasty had a vast territory, developed economy, prosperous culture, and frequent foreign exchanges, which greatly influenced the culture of neighboring countries.

At the end of the Tang Dynasty, national politics continued to corrupt, and the An-Shi Rebellion and the Huangchao Peasant Uprising broke out, which intensified the decline of the Tang Dynasty. In 907 AD, the Tang Dynasty collapsed after 290 years of existence.

Modern China

In 1840, when the Opium War broke out, China began to degenerate into a semi-colonial and semi-feudal society, and the modern history of China began. During this period of history, a series of revolutionary movements and wars took place in China. The more iconic events included the Revolution of 1911 (Xinhai Revolution) and the War of Resistance Against Japanese Aggression.

唐朝

隋末贵族李渊于公元618年建立唐朝,定都长安。之后,在唐太宗李世民的"贞观之治"和中国历史上唯一的女皇武则天的有效治理的基础上,唐玄宗力行改革,国家实力达到鼎盛,史称"开元盛世"。此时的唐朝疆域辽阔,经济发达,文化繁荣,对外交流频繁,极大地影响了周边国家的文化。

唐朝末年,国家政治持续腐败,先后爆发了安史之乱和黄巢农民起义,加速了唐朝的衰落。公元907年,存在了290年的唐朝覆灭。

近代中国

1840年,鸦片战争爆发,中国开始沦为半殖民地半封建社会,中国近代史至此开启。这段历史中,中国发生了一系列的革命运动和战争,比较有标志性意义的事件包括辛亥革命和抗日战争。

The Revolution of 1911

At the end of the Qing Dynasty, under the influence of domestic political crisis and foreign aggression, the Qing government's rule was faltering. In 1905, Sun Yat-sen and others established the Tong Meng Hui (Chinese Revolutionary League) in Tokyo, Japan, marking that China's bourgeois democratic revolution entered a new stage. After the establishment of the Tong Meng Hui, the revolutionary party launched the Wuchang Uprising in October of 1911 successfully. Since 1911 is the Xinhai Year of the Chinese Lunar Calendar, this revolution is called the "Xinhai Revolution" in history. On New Year's Day in 1912, Sun Yat-sen became the interim president in Nanjing, proclaiming the establishment of the Republic of China.

The Revolution of 1911 was a great bourgeois democratic revolution in modern Chinese history. It overthrew the rule of the Qing Dynasty and ended

辛亥革命

清朝末年,在国内的政治危机和外国(列强)侵略的影响下,清政府的统治摇摇欲坠。1905年,孙中山等人在日本东京成立中国同盟会,标志着中国资产阶级民主革命进入了一个新阶段。同盟会成立后,革命党人于1911年10月发动武昌起义,并取得成功。由于1911年是中国农历辛亥年,历史上称这次革命为辛亥革命。1912年元旦,孙中山在南京就任临时大总统,宣告中华民国成立。

辛亥革命是中国近代史上一次伟大的资产阶级民主革命,它推翻了清王朝统治,结束了中国两千

China's feudal monarchy system which has a history of more than 2,000 years. However, due to the weakness and compromise of the bourgeoisie, the Revolution of 1911 did not completely change the nature of China's semi-colonial and semi-feudal society, and the fruits of the revolution were stolen by Yuan Shikai.

The War of Resistance Against Japanese Aggression

On September 18, 1931, Japan instigated the September 18th Incident and occupied the entire territory of Northeast China. The Chinese people rose up to resist, which became the starting point of the War of Resistance Against Japanese Aggression and at the same time opened the prelude to the world's anti-fascist war. In 1935, Japan instigated the North China Incident in an attempt to further occupy China. On July 7, 1937, the Japanese bombarded Wanping County and attacked Lugou Bridge, marking that Japan started a full-scale war of aggression against China. The Chinese soldiers and civilians rose up to counterattack. China thus entered the stage of the nationwide war of resistance and opened up the main eastern battlefield of the world's anti-fascist war.

In the early days of the War of Resistance Against Japanese Aggression, the Nationalist government organized several battles on the frontal battlefield to fight against the Japanese invaders. However, due to the implementation of the one-sided anti-Japanese line, China lost a large area of its territory. The Chinese Communist Party implemented the overall anti-Japanese line and implemented the policy of protracted

多年的封建君主专制制度。然而，由于资产阶级的软弱性和妥协性，辛亥革命并没有彻底改变中国半殖民地半封建社会的性质，革命的胜利果实被袁世凯窃取。

抗日战争

1931年9月18日，日本发动九一八事变，侵占中国东北全境。中国人民奋起抵抗，成为抗日战争的起点，同时揭开了世界反法西斯战争的序幕。1935年，日本制造华北事变，企图进一步占据中国。1937年7月7日，日本炮轰宛平县城，进攻卢沟桥，标志着日本发动全面侵华战争，中国军民奋起反击，中国由此进入全民族抗战阶段，并开辟了世界反法西斯战争的东方主战场。

抗日战争初期，国民政府在正面战场组织多次战役，抗击日本侵略者。但由于实行片面抗战的路线，中国失去大片领土；中国共产党实行的是全面抗战的路线，执行持久抗战的方针。八路军、新四军深入敌后，广泛开展游击战争，建立了许多抗日根据地。

resistance. The Eighth Route Army and the New Fourth Army went deep behind the enemy line, carried out extensive guerrilla warfare, and established many anti-Japanese base areas.

After the Japanese occupation of Guangzhou and Wuhan in October, 1938, the War of Resistance Against Japanese Aggression entered a stalemate. On August 15, 1945, the Japanese government announced its unconditional surrender, and signed an unconditional surrender agreement on September 2. After fourteen years of hard fight, the Chinese people won a great victory in the War of Resistance Against Japanese Aggression, which is an important part of the world's anti-fascist war and has made a significant contribution to the victory of the world's anti-fascist war.

Contemporary China

Since the founding of the People's Republic of China on October 1, 1949, China has entered a period of socialist revolution and construction.

Founding of the People's Republic of China

In September 1949, the first plenary meeting of the Chinese People's Political Consultative Conference was held in Beiping. The conference decided to establish the People's Republic of China. *The Common Program of the Chinese People's Political Consultative Conference* adopted by the conference stipulates that the People's Republic of China is a new democracy, that is, a people's democratic country. The meeting decided to change Beiping to Beijing, the capital of New China, with the five-star red flag as the national flag and *Volunteer March* as the national anthem.

1938年10月，日军占领广州、武汉后，抗日战争进入相持阶段。1945年8月15日，日本政府宣布无条件投降，9月2日签订无条件投降书。经过十四年艰苦奋战，中国人民取得抗日战争的伟大胜利。中国抗日战争是世界反法西斯战争的重要组成部分，为世界反法西斯战争的胜利做出了巨大贡献。

现代中国

自1949年10月1日中华人民共和国成立以来，中国进入了社会主义革命和建设时期。

中华人民共和国的成立

1949年9月，中国人民政治协商会议第一次全体会议在北平举行。会议决定成立中华人民共和国。会议通过的《中国人民政治协商会议共同纲领》规定：中华人民共和国为新民主主义，即人民民主（专政）的国家。会议决定改北平为北京，为新中国的首都，以五星红旗为国旗，以《义勇军进行曲》为国歌。

On October 1, the Central People's Government held its first plenary meeting and the state leaders announced their inauguration. Then, the founding ceremony of the People's Republic of China was held in Tian'anmen Square, announcing the establishment of the Central People's Government of the People's Republic of China.

The founding of the People's Republic of China marked a new era in Chinese history, and the Chinese nation began to stand on its own among the nations of the world with a brand-new outlook.

Reform and Opening-up

After the founding of New China, socialist construction developed tortuously in the course of exploration. As China's economic, cultural and educational work urgently needs to be restored, at the end of 1978, the Central Committee of the Communist Party of China held the Third Plenary Session of the 11th Central Committee in Beijing. The plenum determined the guidelines for seeking truth from facts, affirmed the discussion on the standard of truth, and made the strategic decision to shift the focus of the party and the country's work to economic construction and implement reform and opening-up.

The reform and opening-up began in rural areas, and the nationwide extension of the household contract responsibility system with joint output was realized, which promoted the development of agriculture. The rural reform had promoted the reform of the urban economic system and developed a single public-owned economy into a multi-ownership economy with the public-owned economy as the mainstay. In addition, China has

10月1日,中央人民政府举行第一次全体会议,国家领导人宣布就职。然后在天安门广场隆重举行中华人民共和国开国大典,宣告中华人民共和国中央人民政府成立。

中华人民共和国的成立标志着中国历史进入一个新纪元,中华民族开始以崭新的姿态自立于世界民族之林。

改革开放

新中国成立之后,社会主义建设在探索中曲折发展。因为中国的经济、文化、教育工作亟待恢复,1978年底,中共中央在北京召开十一届三中全会。全会确定了实事求是的指导方针,肯定了真理标准问题的讨论,做出把党和国家的工作重心转移到经济建设上来,实行改革开放的战略决策。

改革开放首先从农村展开,实现了家庭联产承包责任制的全国推广,推动了农业的发展。农村改革推动了城市经济体制改革,把单一的公有制经济发展为以公有制经济为主体的多种所有制经济。此外,中国迈出了对外开放的步伐,通过设置经济特区和开放沿海

taken steps to open up to the outside world, and has promoted rapid economic development through measures such as the establishment of special economic zones and the opening of coastal cities.

Over the past 40 years of reform and opening-up, China's achievements have attracted worldwide attention. China's national economy has continued to develop at a high speed, people's livelihood has been greatly improved, the pace of industrial development has accelerated, and the innovation of the basic system of socialism with Chinese characteristics has been realized.

城市等措施促进了经济的飞速发展。

改革开放40多年来，中国所取得的成就举世瞩目。中国的国民经济持续高速发展，民生大幅度改善，工业发展速度加快，实现了中国特色社会主义基本制度的创新。

Exercises:

I. Questions

1. What are the two most prosperous dynasties in ancient Chinese history?
2. What is the significance of the Revolution of 1911?
3. When did China's reform and opening-up begin? What achievements have been made?

II. Group Discussion

1. Why did the dynasties of ancient China eventually end up?
2. Which dynasty in ancient China are you most interested in? Why?

Suggested Reading:

China's History, written by Cao Dawei and Sun Yanjing, was published by the China Intercontinental Press. This book outlines the development trajectory of Chinese history, represents the demeanor and characteristics of Chinese civilization, and interprets the secrecy of the continuity and rejuvenation of the densely populated ancient civilization after several thousand years of vicissitudes.

第二课 地理概况
Lesson 2 An Overview of Geography

Geographical Location of China

China is located in the east of Eurasia, the largest continent on the earth, and on the west of the Pacific Ocean. The longitude range of China is approximately 73 degrees east longitude to 135 degrees east longitude; the latitude range is approximately 3 degrees north latitude to 53 degrees north latitude. China is bordered by 14 countries on land, including Democratic People's Republic of Korea in the east, Mongolia in the north, Russia in the northeast, Kazakhstan, Kyrgyzstan and Tajikistan in the northwest, Afghanistan, Pakistan, India, Nepal, Bhutan in the west and southwest, and Laos, Myanmar and Vietnam in the south. At the same time, China has a coastline of more than 18,000 kilometers and has many islands of various sizes. China's maritime neighbors are mainly Korea, Japan, the Philippines, Brunei, Malaysia and Indonesia.

Administrative Divisions of China

According to the provisions of *the Constitution of the People's Republic of China*, China's administrative regions are divided as follows:

(1) The country is divided into provinces, autonomous regions and municipalities;

(2) Provinces and autonomous regions are divided into cities, counties, autonomous prefectures and autonomous counties;

(3) Counties and autonomous counties are divided into townships, ethnic group townships and towns.

中国的地理位置

中国位于地球最大的大陆——亚欧大陆的东部，东临太平洋。中国的经度范围大约为东经73度至东经135度；纬度范围大约为北纬3度至北纬53度。中国在陆地上与14个国家接壤，包括东部的朝鲜，北部的蒙古，东北部的俄罗斯，西北部的哈萨克斯坦、吉尔吉斯斯坦和塔吉克斯坦，西部和西南部的阿富汗、巴基斯坦、印度、尼泊尔、不丹，以及南部的老挝、缅甸和越南。同时，中国有长达一万八千多千米的海岸线，并且拥有众多大小不一的岛屿。中国的海上邻国主要有韩国、日本、菲律宾、文莱、马来西亚和印度尼西亚。

中国的行政区划

根据《中华人民共和国宪法》的规定，中国的行政区域划分如下：

（一）全国分为省、自治区和直辖市；

（二）省和自治区分为市、县、自治州和自治县；

（三）县和自治县分为乡、少数民族乡和镇。

There are currently 34 provincial administrative regions in China, including 23 provinces, 5 autonomous regions, 4 municipalities, and 2 special administrative regions.

Provinces

Province as the administrative unit of China originated from the Yuan Dynasty, which has been in use for more than 700 years. There are currently 23 provinces in China (including Taiwan). (Diagram 1.1)

目前中国有34个省级行政区，包括23个省、5个自治区、4个直辖市和2个特别行政区。

省

省作为中国的行政单位源自元朝，至今已经被沿用了七百多年。中国目前共有23个省（包含台湾）。(见表1.1)

Diagram 1.1 Provinces, and Their Abbreviations and Provincial Capitals

Provinces	Abbreviations	Provincial Capitals
Hebei	Ji	Shijiazhuang
Shanxi	Jin	Taiyuan
Liaoning	Liao	Shenyang
Jilin	Ji	Changchun
Heilongjiang	Hei	Harbin
Jiangsu	Su	Nanjing
Zhejiang	Zhe	Hangzhou
Anhui	Wan	Hefei
Fujian	Min	Fuzhou
Jiangxi	Gan	Nanchang
Shandong	Lu	Jinan
He'nan	Yu	Zhengzhou
Hubei	E	Wuhan
Hu'nan	Xiang	Changsha
Guangdong	Yue	Guangzhou
Hainan	Qiong	Haikou
Sichuan	Chuan or Shu	Chengdu
Guizhou	Qian or Gui	Guiyang
Yunnan	Dian or Yun	Kunming
Shaanxi	Shaan or Qin	Xi'an
Gansu	Gan or Long	Lanzhou
Qinghai	Qing	Xining
Taiwan	Tai	Taipei

(The data in this table comes from the statistical table of administrative divisions of the People's Republic of China, December 31, 2018)

Autonomous Regions

Being different from other provincial-level administrative regions, autonomous regions have a large population of ethnic groups, and their local governments have a higher degree of autonomy in managing the internal affairs of their own ethnic groups. China currently has five autonomous regions. (Diagram 1.2)

自治区

自治区与其他省级行政区的主要区别是：少数民族人口聚居量大，且其地方政府在管理本民族内部事务时有较高的自主权。中国目前共有五个自治区。(见表1.2)

Diagram 1.2 Autonomous Regions, Their Abbreviations and Provincial Capitals

Autonomous Regions	Abbreviations	Provincial Capitals
Inner Mongolia Autonomous Region	Inner Mongolia	Hohhot
Guangxi Zhuang Autonomous Region	Gui	Nanning
Tibet Autonomous Region	Tibet	Lhasa
Ningxia Hui Autonomous Region	Ning	Yinchuan
Xinjiang Uygur Autonomous Region	Xin	Urumchi

(The data in this table comes from the statistical table of administrative divisions of the People's Republic of China, December 31, 2018)

Municipalities

Municipalities are provincial-level administrative units established by the Chinese central government to manage strategic cities with political, economic, and geographical advantages more efficiently. There are currently 4 municipalities in China. (Diagram 1.3)

直辖市

直辖市是中国中央政府为了更高效地对具有政治优势、经济优势和区位优势的战略城市进行管理而设立的省级行政单位。中国现有4个直辖市。(见表1.3)

Diagram 1.3 Municipalities, Their Abbreviations and Established Years

Municipalities	Abbreviations	Established Years
Beijing	Jing	1949
Tianjin	Jin	1949
Shanghai	Hu	1949
Chongqing	Yu	1997

(The data in this table comes from the statistical table of administrative divisions of the People's Republic of China, December 31, 2018)

Special Administrative Regions

The special administrative regions are administrative regions established by the central government in accordance with the provisions of *the Chinese Constitution* and actual national conditions. As provincial-level administrative regions, the special administrative regions enjoy a high degree of autonomy, but do not enjoy national sovereignty. At present, China has two national first-level special administrative regions. (Diagram 1.4)

特别行政区

特别行政区是中央政府根据中国《宪法》规定和实际国情设立的行政区域。作为省级行政区,特别行政区享有高度的自治权,但不享有国家主权。目前,中国有两个国家一级特别行政区。(见表1.4)

Diagram 1.4 Special Administrative Regions, Their Abbreviations and Established Years

Special Administrative Regions	Abbreviations	Established Years
Hong Kong	Gang	1997
Macao	Ao	1999

(The data in this table comes from the statistical table of administrative divisions of the People's Republic of China, December 31, 2018)

Topography of China

China has a variety of terrain types, comprehensively including five main terrains of mountains, plateaus, hills, basins and plains. China has a vast area of mountainous areas (including mountains, hills and plateaus), accounting for about 2/3 of the country's area. The terrain of China is high in the west and low in the east in general, and can be divided into three staircases:

The first stair is the Qinghai-Tibet Plateau, with an average altitude of more than 4,000 meters, known as the "roof of the world". Mount Qomolangma, the main peak of the Himalayas on the Qinghai-Tibet Plateau, is 8848.86 meters above sea level and is the world's highest peak.

中国的地形与地势

中国地形多样,全面地包括了山地、高原、丘陵、盆地和平原五种主要地形。中国山区(包括山地、丘陵和高原)面积广大,约占全国面积的2/3。整体来看,中国地势西高东低,分为三个阶梯:

第一阶梯为平均海拔在4,000米以上,有"世界屋脊"之称的青藏高原。这里有喜马拉雅山脉的主峰,世界第一高峰——珠穆朗玛峰,海拔为8848.86米。

The second stair is dominated by plateaus and basins, with an average altitude of 1,000 meters to 2,000 meters. The lowest point of the Turpan Basin is -154 meters above sea level, the lowest point of Chinese land.

The third stair is mostly 500 meters or less above sea level, with many plains, hills and low mountains. From north to south, there are Northeast Plain, North China Plain, and the Middle-Lower Yangtze Plain, known as "The Three Great Plains of China".

Climate of China

China has a vast territory with 50 degrees of latitude spanning from north to south, covering five temperature zones: cold temperate zone, middle temperate zone, warm temperate zone, subtropical zone and tropical zone. Therefore, the climate in different regions of China varies greatly. For example, the average winter temperature in Mohe City, Heilongjiang Province, is close to -30℃, while the average winter temperature in Sanya City, Hainan Province, is above 20℃. Due to the influence of sea and land location, China has a significant monsoon climate. Therefore, the main characteristics of China's climate are four distinct seasons, high temperature and rain in summer, and a cold and dry winter. At the same time, there are significant differences in precipitation in different regions of China.

第二阶梯以高原和盆地为主，平均海拔为1,000米到2,000米。其中吐鲁番盆地最低处海拔为-154米，是中国陆地最低点。

第三阶梯的大部分地区海拔在500米以下，主要分布着平原、丘陵和矮山。从北向南分布着东北平原、华北平原和长江中下游平原，被称为"中国三大平原"。

中国的气候

中国疆域广阔，南北跨越纬度50度，涵盖了寒温带、中温带、暖温带、亚热带和热带5个温度带。因此，中国不同地区的气候有很大差异。例如，黑龙江省漠河市的冬季平均气温接近零下30℃，而海南省三亚市的冬季平均气温为20℃以上。由于受海陆位置影响，中国季风气候显著。因此，中国气候主要特点是四季分明，夏季高温多雨，冬季寒冷干燥。同时，中国不同地区的降水量差异明显。

Resources of China

Water Resources

Rivers and lakes are China's main freshwater resources. China's total water resources are abundant, but due to its large population, water resources per capita are only a quarter of the world average. At the same time, China's water resources are unevenly distributed, and water resources in the west and north are relatively scarce. The Chinese government is constantly optimizing the allocation of water resources and promoting the coordinated development of the region through the implementation of policies such as "South-to-North Water Transfer" and water pollution control.

There are two major rivers in China, the Yangtze River and the Yellow River. The main stream of the Yangtze River is about 6,387 kilometers long and is the longest river in China. It flows through 8 provinces, 1 autonomous region and 2 municipality. It is one of the main arteries of water transportation between eastern and western China and called as the "Golden Waterway". The second longest river in China is the Yellow River, with a total length of about 5,464 kilometers in its main stream, which is the most sediment-heavy river in the world. The Yellow River alluvial plain area is an important base for grains in China, so it is also called as the "Mother River".

China is a country with many lakes, most of which are located in the middle and lower reaches of the Yangtze River and the Qinghai-Tibet Plateau. The middle and lower reaches of the Yangtze River are dominated by freshwater lakes, such as Tai Lake, Poyang Lake and Dongting Lake, etc., and the Qinghai-Tibet Plateau is the main distribution area of saltwater

中国的资源

水资源

河流和湖泊是中国主要的淡水资源。中国的水资源总量丰富，但由于人口数量庞大，人均水资源占有量仅为世界平均水平的四分之一。同时，中国的水资源地域分布不均，西部和北部水资源较为缺乏。中国政府通过实施"南水北调"、治理水污染等政策，来不断优化水资源配置、促进区域的协调发展。

中国有两大主要河流：长江和黄河。长江干流全长约6,387千米，是中国最长的河流。它流经8个省、1个自治区和2个直辖市，是中国东西部之间水路运输的主要动脉之一，被称为"黄金水道"。中国第二长河流是黄河，干流全长约5,464千米，是世界上含沙量最多的河流。黄河的冲程平原是中国粮食生产的重要基地，也因此被称为"母亲河"。

中国是一个拥有众多湖泊的国家，大部分湖泊分布于长江中下游地区和青藏高原地区。长江中下游地区以淡水湖为主，如太湖、鄱阳湖和洞庭湖等；青藏高原是咸水湖的主要分布区，包括青海湖、纳木错湖和奇林科湖等。中国湖

lakes, including Qinghai Lake, Namco Lake and Qilinco Lake, etc.. The distribution of lake water in China shows a trend of decreasing from south to north, and gradually decreasing from east to west. In the humid eastern plains, the lake water is abundant, and in the arid and semi-arid areas in the northwest, the lake water is relatively scarce.

Land Resources

China has a vast land area and large total land resources, but its per capita occupation is small, and especially its per capita cultivated area is relatively small. In 2017, China's per capita arable land area was less than 1.5 mu, less than 1/2 of the world average. In 2019, China's per capita forest area was only 1/5 of the world average. As China continues to strengthen the protection and management of forest resources, as of 2021, China's forest coverage rate had reached 24.02%. In addition, in order to solve the contradiction between urbanization construction land and cultivated land and forest land, China has issued a series of related policies to protect cultivated land and forest land from illegal occupation of construction land by legal means.

Mineral Resources

China has a rich variety of mineral resources, but the structure of resource types is uneven. In terms of energy minerals, China is rich in coal resource, which is China's main energy source; however, China's natural gas, oil and other resources have fewer reserves, and need to rely on imports. In terms of metal minerals, China is the largest producer of iron ore, but most of the iron ore is poor, so China still needs to import a

泊水（资源）的分布呈从南向北递减的趋势，并由东向西递减。在潮湿的东部平原，湖泊水（资源）丰富，而在西北的干旱和半干旱地区，湖泊水（资源）相对稀缺。

土地资源

中国国土面积辽阔，土地资源总量大，但人均占有量小，尤其是人均耕地面积较少。2017年，中国人均耕地面积不足1.5亩，不到世界平均水平的1/2。2019年，中国人均森林面积仅为世界平均水平的1/5。随着中国不断加强森林资源的保护和管理，2021年，中国森林覆盖率已达到24.02%。另外，为了解决城市化建设用地与耕地、林地的矛盾，中国出台了一系列相关政策，以法律的手段保护耕地和林地不被建筑用地违法侵占。

矿产资源

中国的矿产资源种类丰富，但资源类型结构不均衡。能源矿产方面，中国的煤炭资源储量丰富，是中国的主要能源，但中国的天然气、石油及其他资源的储量较少，需要依赖进口。在金属矿产方面，中国是铁矿石第一大生产国，但大多数铁矿为贫矿，所以中国仍然需

large amount to ensure the production and development of the domestic steel industry. (Diagram 1.5)

要通过大量进口来保证国内钢铁工业的生产和发展。(见表1.5)

Diagram 1.5 Remaining Reserves & Resources of Major Minerals in China

No.	Mineral	Unit	2017	2018	Growth Rate(%)
1	oil	billion tons	3.54	3.57	0.9
2	natural gas	billion cubic meters	5522.10	5793.61	4.9
3	coal	billion tons	1666.67	1708.57	2.5
4	iron ore	billion tons	84.89	85.22	0.4
5	cooper	million tons	106.08	114.43	7.9

(The data in this form comes from *the China Mineral Resources 2019* published by Ministry of Natural Resources of the People's Republic of China.)

Animal and Plant Resources

China's rich natural geographical environment provides a good habitat for the survival of various wild animals. In China, there are about 2,070 terrestrial vertebrates, accounting for nearly 10% of the world's terrestrial vertebrates. In addition, China has some rare ancient animals, such as giant pandas, Chinese alligators, and white-fin dolphins. In order to protect these rare wild animals and their habitats, China has established a series of nature reserves.

China has a rich variety of plants, with more than 30,000 plants, ranking third in the world after Malaysia and Brazil. Almost all major plants in the cold, warm and hot temperate zones of the Northern Hemisphere can be seen in China. There are more than 3,000 kinds of plants that can be used for medicine in China.

动、植物资源

中国丰富的自然地理环境为各类野生动物的生存提供了良好的栖息场所。在中国,大约有2,070种陆栖脊椎动物,将近占世界陆栖脊椎动物的10%。另外,中国还生存着一些古老的珍稀动物,如大熊猫、扬子鳄和白鳍豚。为了保护这些珍稀野生动物及其栖息地,中国建立了一系列自然保护区。

中国的植物种类繁多,有30,000多种,仅次于马来西亚和巴西,位居世界第三。在中国几乎可以看到北半球寒温带、暖温带、热带的所有主要植物。中国有超过3,000种可用做药材的植物,长白

Ginsengs in Changbai Mountain, safflowers in Tibet and wolfberries in Ningxia are all valuable traditional Chinese medicine materials.

山人参、西藏红花和宁夏枸杞都是珍贵的传统中药材。

Exercises:

Ⅰ. Questions

1. Can you describe the geographical location of China?
2. What are the first-level administrative regions in China?
3. Which is the longest river in China?

Ⅱ. Group Discussion

1. Do you like the climate in China? Which is your favorite season?
2. In your opinion, what are the differences between China's municipalities and provinces?

Suggested Reading:

1. *Chinese National Geographic Encyclopedia* was written by Zhang Miaodi and published by the Beijing Joint Publishing Co., Ltd. This encyclopedia is based on the administrative divisions of China and covers many aspects of geographic knowledge in all divisions of China.

2. *Atlas of China* was published by the Chengdu Cartographic Publishing House. The content of the book is mainly about maps, accompanied by text descriptions, introducing basic information such as physical geography, social economy of various provinces and regions in China.

Chapter Two
第二章

文学与传统节日
Literature and Traditional Festivals

Introduction

Chinese literature dates back to the hieroglyphs that were used in the Shang Dynasty. It is a vast subject that spans thousands of years. Chinese literary works include fiction, philosophical and religious works, poetry and scientific writings. The dynastic eras frame the history of Chinese literature which is special and unique. This chapter makes an introduction to Chinese literature based on the characteristics.

China has a long history with culture and ideas passed down and expressed in different forms. The traditional festivals of China reflect China's unique cultural heritage. From different festivals, we can find some group activities that all people take part in at specific times. Some are used to celebrate good solar terms, some are used to commemorate great people, and some are used in the hope of getting rid of terrible things.

Learning Goals

1. to have an overall understanding of Chinese literature
2. to learn Chinese classical prose, scientific works, poetry and novels
3. to learn about some famous literary works
4. to know about the main Chinese traditional festivals
5. to learn about different customs of the main Chinese traditional festivals
6. to discuss the legends of the main Chinese traditional festivals

第一课　文学作品
Lesson 1　Literature Works

Chinese Classical Prose

Except for popular novels and theatrical plays, most of the literary prose works were written in the literary classical language. This classical language utilized the grammar and ancient characters of the Warring States Period and of the Han Dynasty era. Writers sought to imitate the philosophical and religious books such as *Mencius* and *Zhuang Zi*. These old texts were thought to contain examples of careful and well-reasoned discourses and be examples of good organizations and styles.

For about 2,000 years after the Qin Dynasty, Chinese writers had a constraint that European writers generally didn't face after the Renaissance. Chinese writers generally needed to write in a common literary language. The ancient languages of the Warring States Period were extinct, but writers had to maintain the grammar and the use of the vocabulary. In some ways, this is similar to how educated Europeans wrote in Latin until the Renaissance era.

During the Han Dynasty, a variant style was developed that was called Piantiwen. This style is ornate and florid. The Piantiwen style was popular for several hundred years afterwards. During the late Tang era, two prominent officials Han Yu and Liu Zongyuan tried to reintroduce the earlier style called Guwen. During the Song Dynasty, another literati named

中国古典散文

除通俗小说和戏剧外，大部分散文作品均以古文书写。此类古文运用了战国时期和汉代的语法及文字。这些作家试图模仿如《孟子》和《庄子》的古代哲学及宗教书籍。这些古文被认为包含论述谨慎、合理的例子，是好的语言组织和风格方面的典范。

秦朝之后的大约两千年里，中国作家面临着一种欧洲作家在文艺复兴之后通常不会面临的限制。中国作家通常需要用一种通用的文学语言来写作。战国时期的古文虽然已经绝迹，但作家们必须保留语法和词汇的用法。在某些方面，这与文艺复兴时期前的欧洲文化人用拉丁语写作类似。

汉代出现了一种变体，被称为骈体文，这种文体较为华丽。此后，骈体文流行了数百年。唐末的两位杰出官员韩愈和柳宗元试图重新引入之前的古文。宋朝，另一位文人欧阳修也帮助复兴古文风格的写作。在随后的八百年中，这种

Ouyang Xiu helped to revive writing in the Guwen style. This neoclassical style dominated prose writing for the next 800 years.

In order to gain entrance into the bureaucracy during the Ming and Qing dynasties, candidates had to pass the imperial qualifying examination. The exam material was the Nine Confucian Classics. The Four Books and Five Classics were memorized by those who did the best on the exams. These works contained the style of writing the literati wished to imitate. After the fourteenth century, vernacular fiction became popular. In the Yuan, Ming and Qing eras, four novels were published that are considered the best in Chinese history. The four novels are called the Four Great Classic Novels of China. All four were written in a vernacular language of their times unlike most ancient literature that was written in the literary classical language.

Chinese Science Works

Chinese science works give an idea of the state of knowledge in the dynastic eras. Gunpowder, printing, the compass, and paper are the "Four Great Inventions of China". The dynastic eras of fastest technological and scientific advancement were the Han and Song eras. The scientific works of the Song era show that the scientists and inventors reached a pinnacle of indigenous development of astronomical, mechanical engineering, alchemical and geographical knowledge. The Han Dynasty mathematical works showed the knowledge of algebra and geometry of that time.

新古典主义风格主导着散文写作。

为了入朝为官,明清时期考生需通过科举考试。考试材料为"九经"。最优秀的考生都能背诵"四书五经",这些著作包含文人喜欢模仿的写作风格。十四世纪以后,白话小说开始流行。元明清时期,"中国古典四大名著"问世,被认为是中国历史上最伟大的四部小说。与大部分以文言文书写的古典文学不同,这四部书是用白话文写成的。

中国科学著作

中国科学著作使人们了解了各个朝代的科技水平。火药、印刷术、指南针和造纸术是"中国(古代)四大发明"。汉代和宋代是科技发展最快的时期。宋代的科学著作表明,当时的天文、机械工程、炼金术和地理领域的科学家及发明家都已掌握了尖端的学科发展知识。汉代的数学著作表明了当时的代数和几何知识水平。

From the Han Dynasty, several mathematical works stood out as achievements. Mathematical works found in Hubei Province can date to about 200 BC. One of these is called *Suan Shu Shu*. It shows how to solve arithmetic problems that officials or people doing business face. A more advanced book called *Jiuzhang Suanshu (Nine-Chapter Computation Book)* is thought to have been written later. The book features basic algebra such as finding cube roots and square roots. Negative numbers are also used. Another mathematical text about astronomical problems compiled during the Han era was *Zhoubi Suan Jing*. The text has a mathematical proof for the "Gougu Theorem" ($a^2+b^2=c^2$).

The second period of rapid scientific and technological advancement was the Song era. Two men in particular stood out. Shen Kuo and Su Song both wrote scientific treatises about their research fields. Shen Kuo's *Dream Pool Essays* of 1088 is a voluminous scientific composition that can be said to contain the forefront of knowledge of his era. He was a world leader in research on the compass and geomagnetism. He is said to have discovered the True North and Magnetic Declination towards the North Pole. He described the magnetic needle compass, which made Chinese sailors sail long distance trips more accurately. One of his essays was about how a printer made and used ceramic movable type for printing texts. He also did advanced astronomical research for his time.

Su Song was one of Shen Kuo's court rivals. He wrote a treatise called the *Bencao Tujing* with information on medicine, botany and zoology. He also made land atlases.

从汉代开始,很多数学著作作为成果脱颖而出。在湖北省发现的数学著作可追溯到约公元前200年。其中之一为《算术书》,它为官员或商人提供解决其所遇到的算术问题的方法。《九章算术》被认为成书较晚,但更完善。其中主要包含求立方根和平方根方面的基础代数知识,还涉及负数的使用。《周髀算经》是汉代编纂的另一本关于天文学问题的数学著作,它证明了"勾股定理"($a^2+b^2=c^2$)。

宋朝是第二个科技迅猛发展的时期,其中有两人尤其突出。沈括和苏颂针对各自的研究领域撰写了很多科学著作。沈括于1088年撰写的《梦溪笔谈》是一部科学长篇著作,可以说包含了当时相关领域最前沿的知识。他是当时世界范围内指南针和地磁学研究方面的佼佼者。据说他发现了"真北"和与北极的"磁偏角"。他对磁针罗盘有所论述,这使中国航海者能更准确地进行长距离航行。他有一篇关于印刷工人制作和使用陶瓷材料的活字印刷术方面的文章。他还从事了就当时来讲较为超前的天文学研究。

苏颂是沈括的同僚,他撰写了专著《本草图经》,记载了医学、植物学和动物学方面的信息。他还制作了地图集。

Chinese Poetry

Poetry has been a favorite literary genre for thousands of years. Especially in the last two hundred years, Chinese ancient poetry is still read and ancient Chinese poets are honored. The greatest poets are thought to have lived a thousand years ago or more during the Tang, Song and Han dynastic eras. There are five major kinds of ancient poetic styles called Shi, Ci, Ge, Qu and Fu.

The structure of the ancient poetry is simpler which is about common things like romance and nature that people appreciate. Since the Chinese have a character-based writing system instead of an alphabetic system, though the language has changed, modern Chinese can still read a lot of ancient poetry.

Five Kinds of Poems

"Shi" is composed of couplets. They are poems of two or more coupled lines. The two lines of a couplet usually rhyme and match rhythmically and complement each other tonally. Modern Mandarin only has four tones, but ancient languages usually had more, so the tonal rhythms are generally lost.

"Ci" can be described as poems that have patterns of syllables and tonal patterns. In making a Ci, a poet chooses words that fit a specific pattern. These patterns may have once been part of a song, but the music has been lost. There are various patterns that provide affective settings for various effects or moods.

The word "Ge" means song. It means the words that can be sung. There were folk songs as well as songs composed by literati and composers.

中国诗歌

数千年来，诗歌一直是最受欢迎的文学体裁。特别是在过去两百年间，人们仍然诵读中国古代诗歌，称颂中国古代诗人。最伟大的诗人被认为生活在一千多年前的唐朝、宋朝和汉朝。主要的五种古诗词类型称作诗、词、歌、曲和赋。

古代诗歌结构较简单，涉及人们珍视的情感和自然等寻常事物。中文基于字符书写系统而非字母，因此即便语言发生了变化，现代中国人仍能读懂许多古代诗歌。

五种诗歌形式

"诗"由对句组成，即两个或两个以上对偶的诗句。对句押韵，在声调上相互补充。现代汉语只有四个声调，而古汉语的声调更多，因此通常古代诗歌在现代汉语中失去了韵律感。

"词"是具有音节和声调模式的诗歌，在词的创作过程中，诗人选择词语来填充特定的模式。这些模式可能曾是歌曲的一部分，但配乐已失传。针对不同的效果或情绪，这些模式具有相应的情感设置。

"歌"即歌曲，是可以被演唱的唱词，包括民歌和文人及作曲家创作的歌曲。

When the Mongols established the Yuan Dynasty, they brought their own style of music and forms of entertainment. They especially liked to watch shadow puppet plays that were little manipulated figurines illuminated by a lamp so that the shadows fell against a screen. It is thought that the form of operatic drama of the Yuan Dynasty imitated their shadow plays. The style of music and song in the operas was called "Yuan Qu", which was also popular in later eras. The poetic style is free of form.

The fifth major style of poetry is called "Fu". They are descriptive poems that contain both prose and couplets. These were popular about 1,500 years to 2,000 years ago. Fu often includes rare or unusual written characters from preceding eras.

Classic Novels

The Four Great Classic Novels of China are usually thought to be the best novels in Chinese literature. The four works were seminal for the development of Chinese societies in past eras. They were widely read by the literati and administrative rulers, and contained philosophical ideas, history, and ideas about human society, family life, and politics that defined part of the world view of the literate in political field. Among these, *Water Margin* and *The Romance of the Three Kingdoms*, are semi-historical, long novels, sort of like *War and Peace* by Tolstoy for impact. *The Dream of the Red Chamber* is reminiscent of a psychologically complex work like Dostoyevskiy's. *Journey to the West* is a mythology filled legendary account which is reminiscent of *Odysseus*.

蒙古人建立元朝后，带来了自己的音乐风格和娱乐形式。蒙古人特别喜欢看皮影戏，受操控的小人像和木偶被灯光照射，影子投射到幕布上。人们认为，元代戏剧是对皮影戏的模仿。戏剧中的音乐和歌曲风格被称为"元曲"，这在之后的朝代也十分流行。这类诗歌形式灵活。

"赋"是第五种主要的诗歌类型，它是包含散文和对句的描述性诗歌。赋流行于大约1,500年至2,000年前。赋经常包括前朝少见或不寻常的书面文字。

古典小说

中国古典四大名著通常被认为是中国文学史上最好的小说。这四部作品对促进中国过去几个朝代社会的发展影响深远。这些书籍被文人和统治者们广泛阅读，书中包含了哲学、历史、人类社会、家庭生活和政治方面的观念，为文学政治领域的世界观形成做出了贡献。其中的《水浒传》和《三国演义》为半历史性长篇小说，其影响力可比托尔斯泰的《战争与和平》。《红楼梦》描写了复杂的心理状态，让人想起陀思妥耶夫斯基的作品。《西游记》充满神话色彩，使人想到《奥德赛》。

Exercises:

Ⅰ. Questions

1. Try to translate a Chinese poem into English.
2. What are the most famous four long novels in China and which novel do you like best?

Ⅱ. Group Discussion

1. Which character in *Journey to the West* is your favorite and why?
2. Which character in *the Dream of the Red Chamber* is your favorite and why?

Suggested Reading:

Chinese Literature was written by Yao Dan and published by Wuzhou Publishing House. The content of the book is mainly about the Chinese literature from the Western Zhou Dynasty to the Yuan Dynasty.

第二课 传统节日
Lesson 2 Traditional Festivals

The Spring Festival

The Spring Festival could be called the most important traditional festival in China. The 1st of January is the beginning of the international year while the Spring Festival is the beginning of a brand-new Chinese year to Chinese people. The Spring Festival takes place during the winter holiday, when the children have finished a semester of courses, the adults have completed a whole year of work, and all the family members are able to gather together. In ancient times, it was said that the Spring Festival was a day when people used to get rid of an evil beast, Nian. People used the huge sounds made by firecrackers to scare off Nian in order to obtain safeness. Now people still gather together for a family reunion dinner. This is the meal where the dishes are the most abundant in the whole year. The Spring Festival is a propitious time which represents peace and reunion however busy they are. During this time, people also come and visit each other to spread happiness. Other activities to celebrate the Spring Festival include giving away red packets to get rid of evils, putting up Spring Festival couplets which represents all the prospects and hopes of the new year, and hanging "Fu" upside down which is a custom coming down from old generations meaning the arrival of good luck.

春节

春节可以说是中国最重要的传统节日。1月1日是国际年的开始，但是对中国人而言，春节才是中国新年的开端。春节在寒假期间来临，此时孩子们结束了一学期的课程，大人们也完成了一整年的工作任务，一家人能够欢聚一堂。在古代，相传春节是人们用来驱除作恶的怪兽——"年兽"的日子。人们用鞭炮的巨大响声吓跑"年兽"，从而获得平安。现在，人们仍然会全家团聚，一起吃一顿整年里最为丰盛的团圆饭。无论多忙，春节都是吉祥的日子，它代表了平安和团圆。在此期间，人们也会互相串门，传递祝福。此外，春节的风俗还有赠送红包——寓意辟邪；贴春联——寓意对新一年的所有展望和期待；从老辈流传下来的挂倒福——寓意福到了。

The Lantern Festival

After the Spring Festival, and also the end of the winter holiday, there is the Lantern Festival. The fifteenth day of the first lunar month is the Lantern Festival, a traditional Chinese festival. The first month is called "yuan", and the ancients called the night "xiao", and the night of this day is the first night with a full moon of the year, so it is called Yuan Xiao Jie in Chinese. People eat Yuanxiao during this time. Yuanxiao is made by wrapping the stuffing in dough and then making the dough into small dumplings to imply reunion. In recent years, there are more varieties of Yuanxiao. It used to be traditional white dumplings, but now different kinds of stuffing are used according to different flavors in various regions. For example, there are osmanthus flavors of Yuanxiao that appear around the areas of Jiangsu Province and Zhejiang Province. In order to suit the preference of different ages, some companies use the dough of different flavors with salty stuffing, sweet stuffing, minced meat or red bean paste. At such a prosperous time of the year, people hang out with one another and go out into the streets to enjoy the lanterns, go shopping at street-side stores, and watch the performance of the dragon and lion dance. In the meantime, to thank Dengshen for bringing light to people, there are events offering incense and praying to Dengshen. Additionally, the Lantern Festival is a romantic festival among the traditional festivals of China. In ancient times, the acquaintance of young men and women was largely dependent on their parents. Parents were afraid that the young men and women would not know each other or meet one another. The Lantern Festival gave young

元宵节

春节之后，寒假之末，就到了中国传统佳节——元宵节，它在农历的正月十五。正月为"元"月，古人称夜为"宵"，而正月十五的夜晚又是一年中第一个月圆之夜，故中文称之为元宵节。人们在元宵节里会吃元宵。元宵是用面团裹住馅料再滚成的小团子，寓意团团圆圆。近年来，元宵的种类变得更多了，以前是传统的小白团子，现在各地会使用不同的馅料做出不同口味的元宵。例如，江浙一带有桂花味的元宵。为了迎合不同年龄层的喜好，一些商家会把元宵做成咸味的或者甜味的，肉末馅的或者红豆沙馅的。在这欣欣向荣的日子里，人们会相约一起在街上观赏花灯，去街边店铺购物，看舞龙舞狮表演。同时，为了感谢灯神带来的光明，也会有给灯神上香祈福的活动。除此之外，元宵节也是中国传统节日中浪漫的一个。在古代，年轻男女的相识大多是由双方父母介绍的，长辈们担心孩子不了解对方情况或没有见过对方，元宵

people an opportunity to meet and get to know each other.

The Dragon Boat Festival

The Dragon Boat Festival is also an important traditional festival. The origin of this festival has two versions with corresponding customs. The first one is that in ancient times, the routine of people's life was to catch fish, shrimps and hunt for prey. When they cooperated to go out for a trip by boat, the hunters would compare with each other the number of water creatures they caught. In their free time, they would also compete to see who could row their boats faster or more steadily. These activities brought a little fun to people's lives. People would even hold small competitions. In such competitions, the person who could row the fastest in the complicated waterway and catch the most fish would win a prize. Actually, the custom of boat-rowing competitions of the Dragon Boat Festival has been initially formed in China since thousands of years ago. However, a boat-rowing competition can only be held in areas with multiple rivers, so this was a unique

节为年轻人提供了一个认识彼此的机会。

端午节

端午节也是一个重要的传统节日，它有两个版本的由来和相应的习俗。第一种说法是：远古时代，人们的日常活动为捉鱼捕虾，追捕猎物。当合作划船捕猎的时候，他们会互相比较捕获水产品的数量。空闲时候他们也会相互比比谁划船更快、更稳。这些活动给人们的生活带来了一丝乐趣。人们甚至会举办小型比赛。在这些比赛中，能在复杂的水道中划船最快、捕鱼最多的人将会获得奖励。其实，端午节龙舟竞技的习俗早在几千年前就已初步形成了。然而，由于划船比赛只能在多河流的地区开展，所以这种习俗是中国南方沿海地区所特有的。可能起初这种习俗只在江浙一带河流多的地

feature of the southern coastal areas of China. It might initially be popular only around the areas of Jiangsu Province and Zhejiang Province where there are many rivers, and later such customs spread to the central and northern areas of China. As a result, the custom of boat-rowing competitions, formed by the river-dwelling people and through the integration of different areas' customs, has become one of the most popular customs on the Dragon Boat Festival.

Others believe that the Dragon Boat Festival was started to commemorate Qu Yuan, who was a great patriotic poet in Chinese history. His ideals and suggestions were not accepted or understood by his emperor, and this ignorance by the monarch would lead to the end of the country. Qu Yuan was so upset that he decided to end his life by drowning himself in a nearby river. Many citizens who respected and supported Qu Yuan, after knowing that he had committed suicide, chose to throw Zongzi into the water hoping to satiate the creatures in the river so that they would not bite the body of the poet and save it from being torn apart. Not only that, but a boat-rowing competition was held hoping to make some noise and stir the water in order to drive away the aquatic life so that they wouldn't damage the body of Qu Yuan.

Both of these tales led to the modern customs of eating Zongzi and holding dragon-boat rowing competitions during this festival. Additional activities derived from these legends include flying paper kites, hanging wormwood and acorus calamus, climbing mountains, drinking realgar wine and so on.

方流行,后来才传到中国中部和北方地区。结果就是,这种由河流部落发源,再和不同地区的习俗融合的龙舟竞技习俗已经成为端午节最受欢迎的习俗之一。

另一种说法认为端午节的由来是为了纪念屈原,他是中国历史上一位伟大的爱国诗人。他的理想和建议没有得到君主的采纳和理解,而这种无视可能最终使国家灭亡,屈原非常沮丧,最终决定投附近的江自尽。那些尊敬和支持他的百姓得知他自杀之后悲痛万分,便向水中投入粽子,希望把水中生物喂饱,不让他的遗体被蚕食。不仅于此,也会举行赛龙舟的活动以发出噪声,搅动水流,赶走水中的生物,避免其对屈原身体的破坏。

这两种说法使得吃粽子和赛龙舟成为如今端午节的风俗活动。另外,由此衍生出来的风俗活动还有放纸鸢,挂艾草和菖蒲,登高,喝雄黄酒,等等。

The Mid-autumn Festival

The Mid-autumn Festival is a festival with a long history. Ancient emperors had the ritual of offering sacrifices to the sun in the spring and the moon in the autumn, which were recorded in the *Rites of Zhou*, a kind of standards and norms which had been taken by the ruling class to maintain their public order. The Mid-autumn happened to be a great and peaceful time which was a symbol of harmony. In order to imitate the rituals of the noble, many literati started to produce works which promoted the Mid-autumn Festival. This led to the celebration of the Mid-autumn Festival among the common folks. Whether it is the great writers enjoying the sight of the moon or worshiping it, expressing their emotions and ambitions through their works about the moon, or the people among the common folks making pastries and lanterns, all these activities reflected people's love for such a great festival. Such kinds of traditional activities became more and more widespread during the Tang Dynasty. The Tang Dynasty was a prosperous dynasty with ample resources where people lived a peaceful and happy life. And it is from the Tang Dynasty that the Mid-autumn Festival became a regular festival. On the Mid-autumn Festival, when the moon is full, people hope to have a reunion with all their family members and gather to enjoy the glorious full moon, eat moon-cakes, and watch the lanterns.

The Qixi Festival

Nowadays, there are all kinds of Valentine's days, and people tend to choose the date which phonetically

中秋节

中秋节历史悠久。古代帝王有春天祭日和秋天祭月的礼制，这种祭日月的风俗在《周礼》一书中就有所记载，《周礼》是统治阶级为了维护他们的公共秩序所采用的标准和规范。而中秋刚好是安静详和的日子，是和谐的象征。为了效仿贵族的礼仪，众多文人墨客开始针对中秋节进行创作，这导致了普通民众也开始庆祝中秋节。无论是大文人观赏、祭拜月亮，借着写月亮的作品抒发感情、表达抱负，还是民间老百姓做糕点、做花灯，所有这些活动都反映出人们对这一重大节日的喜爱。这些传统活动，在唐代就更加普遍了。唐代繁荣昌盛，物阜民丰，人民安居乐业。至此中秋节成为固定的节日。中秋节，月亮正圆，人们也希望在这一天全家团圆，聚在一起赏月，吃月饼，看灯。

七夕

现在，有各种情人节，人们往往会选择日期谐音和爱情相关的

resembles love and emotions to celebrate. For example, May 20th can be a romantic day because it sounds like "I love you" in Chinese. The traditional valentine's day of China is actually the Qixi Festival. There is also a sad but sweet legend about Qixi.

The legend says that, a long time ago, there was a cowherd who lived with an old ox. One day, the old ox told the cowherd to go to the woods where he would see a beautiful fairy. Although the cowherd was very confused, he still went to the woods. Just like the old ox said, this fairy was a beautiful girl (called Zhinv) and they lived a happy life after getting married. However, the happiness didn't last long, the old ox died and Zhinv was taken away by Wangmuniangniang. When the cowherd was chasing his wife, Wangmuniangniang used her hair clasp to make a river in the sky. And the cowherd and Zhinv were therefore separated. They missed each other and cried every day. Finally, the love between them moved the creatures. So, every year on the seventh day of the seventh lunar month the magpies would fly to the river and build a bridge so that they could get reunion. This day of every year is called the Qixi Festival. To commemorate that old ox which helped the cowherd find his true love, in some regions, some people let the cattle out onto the grassland and let them play freely on that day. On this festival, there is a custom of collecting dew. The legend says that, on this day, collecting dew grants the magical power of the moon, which can make people's eyes clear.

Most of China's traditional festivals come from ritual habits and activities for the changing seasons during special solar terms which have existed since our

日子庆祝爱情美满。例如，五月二十日就可以被看作浪漫的日子，因为520在汉语中听起来像"我爱你"的发音。中国的传统情人节实际上是七夕，关于七夕也有一个悲伤而甜蜜的传说。

传说是这样的：很久以前，牛郎与老牛相依为命。一天，老牛让牛郎去树林，说他会在那儿看到一位美丽的仙女。尽管牛郎很纳闷，但还是去了。事情和老牛说得一样，这位仙女是位美丽的姑娘（叫织女）。结为夫妻之后，他们过上了幸福的生活。可是好景不长，老牛死了，织女也被王母娘娘带走了。牛郎紧追妻子之时，王母娘娘用她的簪子划了条天河，牛郎和织女因此被隔开了。他们每日彼此思念，以泪洗面。最后，他们的爱情感动了生灵。于是，每年农历七月初七喜鹊们纷纷飞到天河，搭建天桥，让他们团圆，每年的这一天被称为七夕。为了纪念帮助牛郎找到真爱的老牛，有些地区的人会在这一天把牛群从牛圈里放出来，让它们在草原上自由玩耍。在七夕这一天，人们有收集露水的习俗。传说这一天的露水有月亮的神奇力量，让人眼睛清亮。

多数中国传统节日来源于先祖时期就有的宗教习惯和在特定节气所发生的因季节变换而进行

ancestor's times. The connotation of Chinese cultures is contained in these various festivals. The Spring Festival reflects people's firm faith of a peaceful life and people's resistance to evil and bad things. The Lantern Festival reflects the Chinese people's emphasis on the family reunion. The variety of customs of the Dragon Boat Festival reflects people's commemoration and respect for the hero who made a contribution to history. The Mid-autumn Festival reveals the reunion culture of China. The Qixi Festival shows what romantic love is, and in addition, it reflects people's praise for constant and faithful love and people's hope that every relationship could start well and end well. All of these traditional festivals indicate the long history and profound culture of China and are worth spreading to the world in order to enrich the human civilization. Thus, people are able to enjoy the beauty of life nature and humanity's personalities, sense the firm faith of their lives and enjoy a higher level of their spirits.

的活动，其中蕴含着中国文化内涵。春节代表人们对和平生活的坚强信念和对邪恶事物的反抗；元宵节反映了中国人对家庭团圆的重视；端午节的各种习俗表达了人们对有历史贡献的英雄的纪念和敬重；中秋节显现了中国的团圆文化；七夕节则是人们对浪漫爱情的描绘，也是对专一相守的赞颂和对所有爱情都能善始善终的向往。所有这些传统节日都展现了中国悠久的历史和深厚的文化，值得我们向世界传播，让世界文明更为丰富。如此，人们可以领略到人生的美好和人性的善良，感受到对生命的虔诚，达到更高层次精神境界。

Exercises:

Ⅰ. Questions

1. What do people do on the Lantern Festival?
2. Why do people throw Zongzi into the water on the Dragon Boat Festival?

Ⅱ. Group Discussion

1. Talk about the stories of the Mid-autumn Festival and the Qixi Festival.
2. Describe some other traditional Chinese festivals.

Suggested Reading：

Chinese Feasts & Festivals is a beautiful illustrated Chinese cookbook which features some of the most popular feasts and festival food along with a wealth of information.

Chapter Three
第三章

书画与音乐
Calligraphy, Painting and Music

Introduction

In China, calligraphy and painting occupy distinguished positions in the field of traditional art. They're not only the means of communication, but also the means of expressing a person's inner world in an aesthetic sense. Besides, China has a long and influential history of traditional music, and the core of it is Chinese classical philosophy and culture.

Learning Goals

1. to know about the main characters of Chinese traditional calligraphy
2. to know about major master works in Chinese calligraphy and painting
3. to know about Chinese traditional musical instruments and opera

第一课 书画
Lesson 1 Calligraphy and Painting

Four Treasures of Study

Ancient Chinese people paid great attention to calligraphy. It was essential whereby a candidate could manifest his literary talent in the Imperial Examination, for it gave the first impression to the examiners. Even emperors themselves were good at calligraphy, for example, the versatile Emperor Qianlong in the Qing Dynasty left us many examples of his handwriting on steles in temples and palaces.

Reading books requires studies, and writing brushes, ink sticks, paper and ink stones are called the Four Treasures of Study because they are indispensable in the studies. Among the high-quality treasures, the writing brushes produced in Huzhou, the Xuan paper made in Xuancheng and the ink stones made in Duanxi are the most renowned.

文房四宝

中国古人非常重视书法，因为参加科举考试的考生可以通过做为第一印象的书法来展现自己的文学天分。甚至皇帝自身也很擅长书法，例如：清朝多才多艺的乾隆皇帝在寺庙和宫殿碑石上留下了大量真迹。

读书需要书房，同时"笔墨纸砚"因其在书房中的不可或缺而被称为"文房四宝"。在高品质的珍宝之中，湖州出产的毛笔、宣城出产的宣纸和端溪出产的砚台最为出名。

Writing Brushes

The writing brushes were produced in the Neolithic Age and were used to draw pictures on painted potteries. They were mainly made of the hair of animals. Those made of wool were called Yanghao, and those made of the hair with the tail of weasels were called Langhao. Today's popular pencils, pens, ballpoint pens cannot replace the writing brushes whose unique artistic effects in writing and painting cannot be imitated by any other pens.

Ink Sticks

The ink sticks are the pigment used in writing and painting and they are produced in different places with various kinds. The ink sticks produced in Huizhou are of high quality. A story goes like this, Xi Chao and his son Xi Tinggui, two craftsmen famous for making ink sticks in the Southern Tang Dynasty, were greatly appreciated by the Emperor Li Yu in the Southern Tang Dynasty, who granted their whole family the surname "Li" because they produced a kind of high-quality ink sticks. From then on, the fame of the Li Ink Sticks was widespread. In the Song Dynasty, the name of Shexian, the producing area of Li Ink Sticks, was changed into Huizhou, the Li Ink Sticks were then referred to as the Hui Ink Sticks (the ink sticks produced in Huizhou).

Paper

Paper is among the four great inventions in ancient China. It was first made in the Han Dynasty and then it was greatly refined by Cai Lun. The famous Xuan paper came into existence in the Sui and Tang dynasties. Xuan paper is reputed worldwide as "paper

毛笔

人们在新石器时代就开始制作毛笔,用于在彩陶上作画,这些毛笔主要由动物的毛发制成。用羊毛制成的毛笔被称为羊毫,用黄鼠狼尾毛制成的毛笔被称为狼毫。当今流行的铅笔、钢笔、圆珠笔都无法替代毛笔,毛笔在书画表达上具有独特的、任何其他的笔都无法模仿的艺术效果。

墨

墨是书画颜料,多地有出产,品种多样。徽州生产的墨品质高。有则故事是这样的:希超、希廷珪父子是南唐时期闻名的墨工,受到南唐皇帝李煜的极大赏识,后因制造出一种高品质的墨而整个家族被赐姓"李"。自此,"李墨"名扬天下。到了宋代,"李墨"的产地歙县改称徽州,"李墨"至此被称为"徽墨"(徽州生产的墨)。

纸

纸是中国古代四大发明之一。造纸术最早可追溯到汉朝,后由蔡伦大幅改进。著名的宣纸诞生于隋唐时期。宣纸质地柔软、色白、吸水性好且平滑,因此在世界

that can last for one thousand years" due to its flexible texture, white color, good water-absorbing quality and smoothness.

Ink Stones

As the tool used for grinding the pigment in writing and painting, ink stones were already popular in the Han Dynasty. The Ming and Qing dynasties witnessed the great variety of ink stones as well as the appearance of the Four Famous Ink Stones—Duan Ink Stones, She Ink Stones, Tao Ink Stones and Chengni Ink Stones. They can not only be used in writing and painting but also for admiration due to their exquisite workmanship and attractive appearance.

The Four Treasures of Study are not only stationery with use value but also works of art combining painting, calligraphy and carving. The Palace Museum in Beijing has collected many precious and imperial Four Treasures of Study made with selected materials and exquisite workmanship, representing the highest quality of stationery during the thousands of years in Chinese history.

Formation of Chinese Characters

There are five general styles that are traditionally used in Chinese calligraphy, which are Zhuan Shu, Kai Shu, Xing Shu, Li Shu, and Cao Shu. Each of these has its own special characteristics, and is derived from different origins dating back to different dynasties.

Zhuan Shu (Seal Characters)

This style gets its name from the ancient characters used in official seals. Seal characters are very popular with calligraphy artists for their elegant style and are divided into both small seal and big seal characters. Small seal characters are also known as Qin Seal. Small seal characters are simpler and more standard than big seal ones.

Big seal characters have their foundation in oracle bone inscriptions which can be dated back to the Zhou Dynasty.

Kai Shu (Formal Script)

Kai Shu, otherwise known as Zheng Shu script, evolved from seal characters. Kai Shu is known for its squareness, and horizontally and vertically standardized structure. Its simplicity makes it a neat and orderly way of writing, which is possibly the reason why it is also very popular among calligraphers.

篆书

这种字体得名于它是古代官印上所刻的字的字体。其风格典雅，广受书法家的欢迎，可分为小篆和大篆。小篆也称秦篆。小篆比大篆更简洁、更规范。

大篆以甲骨文为基础，可追溯到周朝。

楷书

楷书也称正书，由篆书演变而来。楷书因其字体方正，上下、左右结构规范为人们所知。它的简单使其书写起来整齐划一，这可能也是其颇受书法家欢迎的原因。

（篆书）

（楷书）

Xing Shu (Running Script)

Xing Shu is the cursive form of Kai Shu, thereby making it a very quick, convenient and practical way of writing. It looks very much like Kai Shu. Xing Shu comes from the Han Dynasty.

Cao Shu (Cursive Hand)

As another cursive form of calligraphy, Cao Shu also goes back to the Han Dynasty. Although it had its origins with the Western Han Dynasty, it did not become popular until the Eastern Han Dynasty. Cursive Hand is very simple, irregular and sketchy, yet highly artistic.

Li Shu (Official Script)

The strongest characteristic of Li Shu is its diversity. Although it has a neat look, it is a more complex type of writing with its different variations. Li Shu became the writing which eventually transitioned into formal script.

An interesting story goes like this: Wang Xizhi stressed getting inspiration from nature and said, "a goose is the hero of poultry because it is as white as snow and as clean as jade". Therefore, he loved to observe the movements of geese to think about how to wield his writing brush. One morning when Wang enjoyed the landscape scenery on boat, he was unconsciously absorbed in watching the white geese on the opposite bank and wanted to buy these geese. The owner of the geese was a Taoist who said, "if you want to get these geese, please write for me *The Yellow Court Classic* as for Taoists to keep in good health!" Wang

行书

行书是楷书的草化，因此行书书写快捷、方便且实用。它看起来和楷书很像。行书源自汉代。

草书

作为另外一种草写体的书法形式，草书也可追溯到汉代。虽然草书起源于西汉，但直到东汉才开始流行。草书非常简单、不规则且粗略，但极富艺术感。

隶书

隶书的最大特点是多变。隶书看似齐整，但变体多，因此书写风格更为复杂。隶书最终演变为正式书写字体。

有则故事很有趣：王羲之想从大自然中汲取灵感，他说："鹅为禽中豪杰，白如雪、洁如玉。"因此，他喜欢观察鹅的举动，以此来思考如何运笔。一日清晨，王羲之在船上欣赏风景，不觉被对岸的白鹅们所吸引，想将它们买下。鹅主是一位道士，说道："请为我抄写一份祈求道士健康的《黄庭经》来换这些鹅！"王羲之太想得到鹅了，于是欣然答应，以其书法作品换取了白鹅。

Xizhi was so desperate to get the geese that he agreed and exchanged his calligraphy work for the white geese.

Even to this day, Chinese people still love and use calligraphy. The calligraphy does not lose its charm but attracts many foreigners. Calligraphy displays, explanations and practice are seen both in international education courses of Chinese characters and cultural events in Confucius Institutes overseas.

Guo Hua (Traditional Chinese Painting)

Guo Hua refers to the paintings drawn on silk or paper by writing brushes in water, ink or color. The subjects include human figures, landscapes and flowers and birds. In fact, they are categorized based on their artistic expression concepts and thoughts although they seem to be classified according to their subjects. Human figure paintings reveal everything in the world as well as interpersonal relationships; landscape paintings combine humans and nature and reveal the harmony between them; flower and bird paintings depict all creatures in nature and demonstrate the vigor and vitality of the universe. The techniques can be divided into fine brushwork, freehand brushwork and so on. The traditional Chinese paintings reflect Chinese people's understanding of nature and human society in a representational way. Mountains, rivers, plants, animals, etc. can all be chosen for their traditional association as much as for their inherent beauty.

In Chinese people's minds, the plum of blossom, orchid, bamboo, and chrysanthemum are known as four gentlemen in Chinese classic literature. They are not only four plants, but also present the four seasons and

直到今天，中国人仍然热爱并使用书法，书法魅力未减，而且吸引了众多外国人。在国际汉字教育课程和海外孔子学院的文化活动中都能看见书法展览、讲解及实践活动。

国画（传统中国绘画）

国画是指用毛笔蘸水、墨或颜料在丝绸或纸上绘制的画作。题材包括人物、风景及花鸟。国画的分类看似基于题材，但实际上却基于艺术表达观念。人物画描绘世界万物及人际关系；山水画将人与自然融为一体，彰显两者的和谐；花鸟画聚焦自然界中所有生物，展现宇宙的生机和活力。按技法分类，国画包括工笔画和写意画等。中国传统绘画以具象的方式反映出中国人对自然和人类社会的理解。山脉、河流、植物、动物等因其传统关联意义及其内在的美均可被选用。

在中国人的观念里，梅、兰、竹、菊是中国古典文学"四君子"。它们不仅仅是四种植物，还代表四季和中国人欣赏的个性及品行。

the personality and conduct Chinese people appreciate. The plum of blossom, stands for bravery and the messenger of spring, the symbol of grace and nobility in Chinese culture; the orchid, a modest flower, stands as the symbol of secluded charm because it is often found in a deserted shady valley; the bamboo symbolizes integrity and simplicity; the chrysanthemum, stands for elegance, righteousness and longevity. Besides, there are another three kinds of plants that are often used as themes of Chinese painting: the pine tree, peony and lotus. The pine tree stands for the uprightness and immortality. The peony presents wealth and honor. The lotus, coming out of the mire without being smeared, stands for kindness, harmony, purity, and both the blooming lotus and the luxuriant lotus leaves symbolize prosperity and continuity.

梅花是春天的信使,代表勇气,是中国文化中优雅、崇高的象征;兰花性情温和,常见于荒凉、幽暗的山谷,因此象征隐世魅力;竹代表正直、朴素;菊花象征着高贵、正气和长寿。此外,有其他三种植物:松树、牡丹和荷花,也常被用作国画主题。松树代表正直和不朽;牡丹代表富贵和荣誉;荷花出淤泥而不染,代表善良、和谐、纯洁,盛开的荷花和茂盛的荷叶都象征着繁荣与延续。

Notable Painters of Traditional Chinese Painting

Gu Kaizhi, an outstanding calligrapher and painter in the East Jin Dynasty, was good at figure painting, animal painting and landscape painting, with representative works like *Ode to the Goddess of the Luo River Painting* and *Admonitions of the Court Instructress to Palace Ladies*.

知名传统国画画家

顾恺之:东晋时期杰出的书法家和画家,擅长人物画、动物画和山水画,其代表作品有《洛神赋图》和《女史箴图》。

Zhan Ziqian, living through the North Qi, North Zhou and Sui dynasties, painted many murals in Luoyang, Chang'an (Xi'an now) and Yangzhou. Among them, the murals of landscape painting take the highest achievement. *Madam Gou's Spring Outing* is a representative work of Zhan Ziqian, and the oldest existing scroll landscape painting of China.

Yan Liben, another master of traditional Chinese painting, was born in a family of painters and roamed widely in calligraphy and painting. His representative works are *Thirteen Portraits for Emperors* and *Bunian Tu*.

Wu Daozi is known as the Sage Painter in Chinese painting history, with representative works like *Born of Gautama Buddha* and *Portrait of Confucius When Teaching*.

Zhang Zeduan was good at drawing buildings, woods and trees and figures, used to work at the Imperial Painting Academy, and created the famous *Riverside Scene at Qingming Festival*.

Li Gonglin was especially good at painting horses.

Shen Zhou, one of the outstanding painters in the Ming Dynasty, was of great learning in literature and poetry.

Zheng Banqiao, a famous painter in the Qing Dynasty, was skilled in drawing plants like orchids, bamboos, chrysanthemums and pine trees.

展子虔：经历了北齐、北周和隋朝，在洛阳、长安（今西安）和扬州绘制了许多壁画，其中的山水壁画达到了最高成就。展子虔的代表作品《虢国夫人游春图》是中国现存最古老的卷轴山水画。

阎立本：中国另一位国画大师，生于绘画世家，广泛进行书画创作。其代表作包括《历代帝王图》和《步辇图》。

吴道子：中国画史尊称其为画圣，代表作品有《天王送子图》和《孔子行教像》。

张择端：擅长绘制建筑、树林、树木及人物，曾供职于皇家画院，创作了著名的《清明上河图》。

李公麟：尤其擅长画马。

沈周：明代杰出画家之一，在文学和诗歌领域造诣颇高。

郑板桥：清代著名画家，擅长画植物，如：兰、竹、菊、松。

Exercises:

Ⅰ. Questions

1. Zhuan Shu, Kai Shu, Xing Shu, Li Shu, and Cao Shu have their own special characteristics. Which one do you like best?
2. What are the traits of the fine brushwork and freehand brushwork?

Ⅱ. Group Discussion

1. What are the plum of blossom, orchid, bamboo and chrysanthemum standing for?
2. What kind of Guo Hua do you like better, fine brushwork or freehand brushwork?

Suggested Reading:

Song Renhua was written by Yang Jianfei and published by China Academy of Art. You can appreciate all kinds of famous paintings from this book.

第二课 音乐
Lesson 2 Music

In Confucian teachings, the purpose and role of music are laid out and the qualities of "good music" are defined. Confucian teachings about how music was meant to be used and performed are expressed in several of the main Confucian books: *Analects* (Lún Yǔ), *The Classic of Poetry* (Shī Jīng), and *the Classic of Rites* (Lǐ Jì). These confucian teachings are seminal for understanding traditional music. Confucius taught that, "To educate somebody, you should start with poems, emphasize ceremonies, and finish with music." Musical knowledge was a matter of higher learning. It is said that he thought that of the six most important subjects to study, and studying music was second in importance only to the study of ritual.

儒家教义阐明了音乐的目的和作用,定义了"好音乐"的特质。多部主要的儒学著作列出了使用和表演音乐的儒家教义,包括:《论语》《诗经》和《礼记》。这些教义对于理解传统音乐具有重大意义。子曰:"兴于诗,立于礼,成于乐"。音乐知识是高级别教育的一部分。据说,他认为,在六艺(礼、乐、射、御、书、数)中,学习音乐的重要性仅次于学习礼节的重要性。

Rite and Ritual

Music is so important because the ideal society is to be governed by rites, ritual and ceremonial functions, but not by law or raw power. In a culture where people function according to ritual and ceremony, music is used to help conduct and govern them. So music isn't only for entertainment, but a means for musicians to accomplish political and social goals. Music is ultimately a means for optimizing social utility and happiness.

General Traits of Traditional Music

Grand Entry

In general, traditional musicians follow the Confucian teachings. In order to perform the grand and "magnificent" entry of musical pieces advocated by Confucius, musicians in an orchestra or ensemble often begin their pieces with a grand flourish of all of them playing their instruments simultaneously for a few seconds or by sounding a gong or drum loudly. This signals that the piece has begun and catches the audience's attention. An instrumental musician performing solo often plays a sudden loud note or notes at the beginning. In a group ensemble, after the grand opening of the piece, the musicians generally tone the volume down towards the middle. This enables the audience to appreciate the technical finesse of the individual musicians. At the conclusion of a piece, the volume generally increases again for the finale. Traditional Chinese music emphasizes the precise elucidation of each note of an instrument, but there isn't an emphasis on rhythm or Western-style harmony.

礼节与仪式

理想社会应受礼节、仪式和礼仪职能的制约,而非律法或蛮力的制约,因此音乐非常重要。在利用仪式和礼仪约束人民的文化中,音乐起到了帮助实施管理的作用。因此音乐并不仅仅是一种娱乐,它还是音乐人完成政治和社会目的的一种手段,最终可以提高社交效用和幸福感。

传统音乐的一般特征

盛大开场

一般而言,传统音乐家遵循儒家教义。为了演奏孔子提倡的盛大开场片段,管弦乐队或合奏团的音乐家通常会齐奏几秒钟,或大声击打锣或鼓。这表明,表演已经开始,以此吸引观众注意。独奏器乐演奏者通常会在开始时,突然大声演奏一个或多个音符;在合奏中,音乐家通常会在音乐隆重开场后,将音调调低到中间位置,这样观众就能欣赏到个人音乐家的精湛技艺。到了一章结束之时,音量通常会再次升高,以谢幕。中国传统音乐强调对乐器每个音符的精确阐释,但不强调节奏或西式的和声。

Pentatonic Scale

Most of the traditional music uses the ancient Chinese pentatonic scale. The scale lends to making simple harmonies, but perhaps to maintain the Confucian norms of simplicity and clarity, harmony isn't emphasized. In contrast, Western-style music uses the heptatonic scale that produces complex harmonies among various instruments.

Smoothly Continuous

Unlike Western music, there is no emphasis on rhythm or beat in traditional Chinese music. As Confucius taught, "beautiful and appropriate music is meant to promote social tranquility."

Grand Finale

In accord with Confucius' idea of music being "smoothly continuous", traditional music generally doesn't have sharp breaks in tempo. However, instead of a regular tempo throughout, many pieces feature a regular but smoothly accelerating tempo. The tempo slowly increases towards a finale at the end. This connotes a river gaining speed as it cascades downwards, and this is often the rhythmic feature of traditional Chinese music.

Three Kinds of Traditional Music

Over the centuries, there are three main styles of classical music performances that you can enjoy in China: Chinese opera music meant for theatrical performances, ensemble or orchestra music for cultured audiences, and solo instrumental performances.

五声音阶

大多数传统音乐使用中国古代五声音阶。此音阶可标注简单和声，但或许是为了保持儒家简洁明了的准则，和声并不被强调。相比之下，西方音乐使用的七声音阶可以使各种乐器产生复杂和声。

平稳连续

与西方音乐不同，中国传统音乐不强调节奏或节拍。如孔子言，优美合适的音乐意在促进社会安宁。

盛大结尾

传统音乐与孔子"平稳连续"的音乐观一致，在节奏上一般没有明显变化。但是，许多乐曲节奏并非全程都很平稳，而是有规律地平缓加速。节奏会慢慢加快，直到演出结束，就像一条河流在奔腾入低处时逐渐加速一样，这通常是中国传统音乐的节奏特征。

三种传统音乐

经过几个世纪的发展，如今在中国仍然可以听到三种主要的古典音乐演奏风格：中国戏曲在剧院中的表演，文艺观众观看的乐团或管弦乐合奏以及乐器独奏。

Chinese Opera Music

Despite the ancient Chinese belief that music was not meant to amuse, but to purify one's thoughts, modern Chinese opera music is meant for entertainment more. There are several types of Chinese opera now, but the favorites are probably Peking Opera and Sichuan Opera. The instruments include erhu and other stringed instruments, wood clappers, gongs, cymbals, and wind instruments. The main function of the stringed instruments is to accompany the singing, but they are used to make special effect sounds such as animal sounds.

Traditional Music Ensembles and Orchestras

Many works of traditional music are still played by ensembles and large orchestras. Nowadays, Chinese musicians in a traditional ensemble incorporate Western and modern musical styles. Even the instruments may be redesigned to play according to Western musical styles and are made from modern materials.

Non-traditional instruments such as a piano may also perform traditional music, so the music doesn't sound exactly like the music played 200 years ago. Western audience is intrigued by the differences in style and sound compared to Western orchestral music.

Peking Opera

Peking Opera is a synthesis of stylized action, singing, dialogue, mime, acrobatic fighting and dancing to represent a story or depict different characters and their feelings of gladness, anger, sorrow, happiness, surprise, fear, sadness and so on. The characters may be

中国戏曲

尽管古代中国人认为音乐非娱乐，而旨在净化思想，但现代中国戏曲却更多以娱乐为目的。目前有多种中国戏曲形式，而最受人喜爱的可能是京剧和川剧。乐器包括二胡和其他弦乐器、木拍板、锣、钹和管乐器。弦乐器的主要功能是为歌唱伴奏，但也用来制造特殊声效，比如动物的声音。

传统合奏团及管弦乐队

合奏团和大型管弦乐队仍在演奏很多传统音乐作品。如今，传统合奏团中的中国音乐家融合了西方和现代音乐风格，甚至可以根据西方的音乐风格，用现代材料重新设计演奏乐器。

非传统乐器如钢琴也可以演奏传统音乐，所以现在的音乐与200年前的音乐听起来已经有所不同。西方听众会被与西方管弦乐不同风格的中国传统音乐激起兴趣。

京剧

京剧是一种程式化的动作、演唱、对话、哑剧、杂技格斗和舞蹈的综合艺术，用于故事重现或描绘不同角色的喜悦、愤怒、懊悔、快乐、惊奇、恐惧、悲伤等情绪。角色或

loyal or treacherous, beautiful or ugly, good or bad. Their images are always vividly manifested in bright costumes that show the styles of ancient China.

There are currently four main role categories in Peking Opera: Sheng, Dan, Jing and Chou, each of which has its own modeling feature and acting system. Sheng means male characters, mainly including laosheng, xiaosheng and wusheng. Dan represents female characters, mainly including laodan, qingyi, huadan and wudan. Jing means male characters with distinct personality and tough bodies such as hero, general and god. Chou is a comical role which is the mostly funny or negative character. Among these roles, the jing's facial makeup is the most well-known and called lianpu. Any role in these categories or sub-categories can be the leading role in a play. Except the second category — Dan, the other three categories are for male characters.

It is said that the reason why the role categories take the names of Sheng, Dan, Jing and Chou is that they were chosen to mean the opposite. Sheng in Chinese may mean "strange" or "rare", but the chief male is the character of the most seen.

Dan, which means "morning" "masculine", is in contrast with the feminine nature of the characters.

Jing means "clean". In fact, the paintings on face make the characters look unclean but colorful.

Chou in Chinese represents the animal "cow", which, in some aspects, is slow and tardy. In contrast, Chou characters are usually active and quick. Peking Opera is different from opera, because the latter tells the stories and expresses the thoughts by singing instead of speaking while the former stresses chang,

诚或奸，或美或丑，或好或坏。其形象总是通过鲜艳的服饰来体现，从而展现出古代中国的风格。

目前，京剧中有生、旦、净、丑四个主要角色类别，它们都有各自的造型特征和表演体系。生指男性角色，主要包括老生、小生和武生。旦代表女性角色，主要包括老旦、青衣、花旦和武旦。净指具有鲜明个性和强健体魄的男性角色，如英雄、将军、神。丑是喜剧角色，主要负责滑稽或反面的角色。其中，净的脸妆最为人们所熟悉，称为脸谱。以上各类别或子类别的任何角色都可以担当戏剧主角。除第二类的旦以外，其他三个类别都为男性角色。

生、旦、净、丑四大角色类别得名的原因据说与各自的含义刚好相反。汉语中生的意思是"陌生"或"罕见"，但男主角却是最常见的角色。

旦意为"早上""男性"，与角色的女性特质相反。

净的意思是"干净"，然而实际上，其脸妆却很显脏，但色彩丰富。

丑在汉语中代表动物"牛"，有些方面，动作缓慢而反应迟缓，但与之相反，丑角人物通常活跃而敏捷。京剧不同于歌剧，后者是通过歌咏而非说话来讲故事和表达思想，而前者则强调"唱、念、做、

nian, zuo, da. Chang refers to singing, nian refers to musical spoken parts, zuo refers to dance movements, and da refers to martial skills. Therefore, Peking Opera is a comprehensive art.

The traditional opera consists of mainly tales of preceding dynasties, important historical events, emperors and empresses, ministers and generals, geniuses and great beauties. They represent stories from the ancient times to Yao, Shun, Yu, the Spring and Autumn Period, the Warring States Period and the dynasties of Qin, Han, Sui, Tang, Song, Yuan, Ming and Qing.

Some of the newer operas were adapted from literature or classical novels during the early days of the founding of New China. Some of the popular stories during the history are *Orphan of Zhao Family*, *Fifteen Strings of Coppers*, *The Ruse of Empty City*, *The Story of the White Snake*, *The Drunken Concubine* and *Unicorn-Trapping Purse*.

As the most recognizable feature of Peking Opera, the costumes are graceful, elegant and brilliant in color and design. They are mostly made using hand sewing and embroidery. As the traditional Chinese patterns are adopted, the costumes are of a high aesthetic value. Makeup and masks are very important to the aesthetic of Peking Opera. The colors are rich and depict different characters using symbolism of color. Black often represents upright and intrepid characters, while white indicates wickedness.

The performance is accompanied by a tune played on wind instruments, percussion instruments and stringed instruments, and the chief musical instruments are Jinghu (a two-stringed bowed instrument with a high register),

打"。"唱"即歌唱,"念"代表说唱部分,"做"代表舞蹈动作,"打"指武术技巧。因此,京剧是一门综合性艺术。

传统戏曲主要包括前朝的故事、重要的历史事件、皇帝和皇后、文臣和武将、天才和美人。故事从远古时代讲到尧、舜、禹,再到春秋、战国时期,以及秦、汉、隋、唐、宋、元、明、清时期。

新中国成立初期,有些较新的戏曲是由古典文学或小说改编而成的。这段历史中,最受欢迎的故事有《赵氏孤儿》《十五贯》《空城计》《白蛇传》《贵妃醉酒》和《锁麟囊》。

作为京剧最显著的特征,服饰色彩和设计优美、雅致且鲜艳。大多采用手工缝制和刺绣。服饰采用中国传统图案,因此具有很高的美学价值。妆容和脸谱是京剧极其重要的审美特征,其色彩丰富,通过不同颜色的象征意义来刻画不同的角色。黑色通常代表正直、勇猛,而白色代表邪恶。

表演伴奏由管乐器、打击乐器和弦乐器完成。主要乐器包括:京胡(高音域二弓弦乐器)、月琴(四弦弹奏乐器,音箱为满月形)、三弦

Yueqin (a four-stringed plucked instrument with a full-moon-shaped sound box), Sanxian (a three-stringed plucked instrument), Suona, flute, drum, big-gong, cymbals, small-gong, etc..

In Peking Opera performance, the interaction between the performers and the audience is also one of the charms of this art. In the past, the stage was often set within the audience. The performers acted on stage and the audience cheered off stage, forming a scene of bustle and excitement. Today, Peking Opera has become the quintessence and the sign of Chinese culture, directly reflecting the rich and profound Chinese culture from one perspective.

Peking Opera v.s. Western Opera

The Performing Style

Western opera focuses on powerful singing and emotional expressions during the performances. The acting is self-explanatory, fluid, and life-like. In Peking Opera, as well as the more stylized singing, each performer's actions are important ways to tell the story. The performance style is more of a symbolic visual show. For example, a performer ties a horsewhip on his wrist, and when he waves the horsewhip, it means he's riding a horse.

The Stage Setup

Peking Opera's stage is normally a simple platform that only has one side exposed to the audience. A Western opera's stage setup is more complicated. The stage normally has vivid and various props.

（三弦弹奏乐器）、唢呐、长笛、鼓、大锣、钹、小锣等。

京剧演出中，表演者与观众的互动也是这门艺术的魅力之一。过去，舞台通常设置在观众中间。表演者在台上演出，观众在台下欢呼，场面热闹非凡。如今，京剧已成为中华文化的精髓和标志，从一个侧面直接反映出中国文化的丰富和深远。

京剧与西方歌剧对比

表演风格

西方歌剧注重表演过程中浑厚的唱腔和情感表达，表演自明、流畅且生动。京剧，除了比较风格化的演唱之外，每名演员的动作也是讲述故事的重要方式。表演风格更加象征视觉化。比如表演者将马鞭绑在他的手腕上，挥起马鞭时，就代表他正在骑马。

舞台设置

京剧舞台形式简洁，只有一面朝向观众。西方歌剧的舞台设置更为复杂，上面通常摆放有各种生动的道具。

The Makeup

A Peking Opera performer's makeup is more complicated than that of a performer in Western opera. A Western opera performer's makeup is closer to real life, while the makeup for Peking Opera is thick and heavy in colors, which symbolizes character roles.

Musical Instruments

In Western opera, often a full orchestra is used, while only traditional Chinese percussion instruments, such as drums and gongs, are used in Peking Opera. Wang Guowei, a Chinese scholar, said that Peking Opera uses singing and dancing to express stories. The story plots emerge as the performers use intoned dialogue and actions.

妆容

相较于西方歌剧,京剧演员的妆容更加复杂。西方歌剧演员的妆容更接近真实生活,而京剧演员的妆容浓厚,色彩浓郁,用来代表不同的角色。

乐器

西方歌剧中常会用到整个管弦乐队,而京剧主要使用传统的中国打击乐器,例如鼓和锣。中国学者王国维曾说过:"戏曲者,谓以歌舞演故事也。"表演者通过吟咏台词和表现动作来推动情节的发展。

Exercises:

Ⅰ. Questions

1. What are the differences between Sheng, Dan, Jing and Chou in Peking Opera?
2. What are the differences between Peking Opera and Western Opera?

Ⅱ. Group Discussion

1. Which Chinese traditional music do you like best?
2. Do you like Chinese opera? And why?

Suggested Reading:

A companion to Chinese traditional music was written by Guo Shuhui and published by Shanghai Musical Publishing House. This book will tell you many details about the Chinese traditional music.

Chapter Four
第四章

自然与人文景观
The Natural Landscapes and Humanity Landscapes

Introduction

China lies in the east of Asia, the west coast of the Pacific Ocean. As a vast country, China covers an area of about 9.6 million square kilometers. Due to its vast territory, the natural landscapes and humanity landscapes are different from each other. The landscapes in some parts of China are magnificent and vigorous, while they are characterized by their beauty and charm in some other places. By means of transportation, people can enjoy different landscapes from Mohe to Nansha Islands only in one day, and that means people can enjoy different landscapes from spring to winter in one day. In this chapter, some representative natural landscapes and humanity landscapes in China are introduced.

Learning Goals

1. can give a brief introduction to the landscapes introduced in this chapter
2. to learn the features of the landscapes introduced in this chapter
3. to enjoy the beauty of different landscapes
4. to learn geography terms and expressions related to the natural landscapes and humanity landscapes

第一课 自然景观
Lesson 1 Natural Landscapes

The West Lake in Hangzhou, Zhejiang Province

The West Lake, one of the most famous tourism highlights in China, is located in Hangzhou, Zhejiang Province. It has been known around the world for its unique scenery and cultural heritage for centuries. The landscape of the whole West Lake is mainly composed of three parts: the nearby mountains, the surrounding landscape relics and the West Lake itself. The lake area is about 60 square kilometers with the water area of about 6.5 square kilometers.

The beauty of the West Lake lies in its picturesque scenery. The overall pattern of the West Lake is "mountain on three sides and city on one side". Its north, west and south sides are closely connected to mountains. The east bank of the West Lake is the west boundary of the urban area of Hangzhou city. The water area of the West Lake is famous for the pattern of "two dikes and three islands". The lake is divided into several regions with different sizes by the Su and Bai dikes and the natural island Gushan. The three islands are interspersed among them, like the Yaotai fairyland, which symbolizes the fairyland image of "one pool and three mountains" in the Qin and Han dynasties. The style of dividing and organizing the space by dike and island, which combines the unique landscape of the lake dike in the south of China, is an outstanding example of how human beings create an elegant

浙江省杭州市西湖

西湖位于浙江省杭州市，是中国最著名的旅游亮点之一。几个世纪以来，它以其独特的风景和文化遗产闻名于世。整个西湖的景观区域主要由三部分构成：附近的山体、四周的景观遗迹以及西湖自身。西湖的湖区面积大概有60平方公里，水域面积约为6.5平方公里。

西湖的美丽，在于它的风景如画。西湖的总体格局为"三面环山一面傍城"。西湖的北岸、西岸和南岸与山脉紧密相连，东岸是杭州城区的西界。西湖以其"两堤三岛"的水域格局而闻名。苏堤和白堤两条长堤以及孤山自然岛将湖区划分为大小不一的区域。三岛点缀其间，如同瑶台仙境，也象征着秦汉以来所流传的"一池三山"的仙境。以堤和岛屿为界，对空间进行合理分割的方式，充分彰显了中国江南地区特有的堤坝风貌，也是人类因地制宜利用古潟湖创造美景的突出代表。这也是中国园林景观设计中的一种重要方法，不但赋予景观更高的美学观赏功能，

environment by using the ancient lagoon. It is also an important architectural style of Chinese landscape design, which not only has the large- scale aesthetic appreciation function, but also enriches the landscape style, highlighting the concept of pursuing harmony between man and nature in eastern culture.

The beauty of the West Lake lies in people's protection and inheritance of history and culture. With its impressive scenery, the West Lake is rich in cultural heritage and legends that passed from generation to generation. Due to its profound history and important historical significance, the West Lake is also a cultural resort with 3 national key historical sites and cultural relics under protection, 10 provincial cultural relics under protection, and 1 municipal cultural relics under protection. Among the whole scenic area, there are more than 100 scenic spots open to tourists at present. Every year, more than 30,000,000 tourists come to Hangzhou to enjoy the beauty of the West Lake.

Shennongjia National Park in Hubei Province

The Shennongjia National Park is a national park that located in Shennongjia forest district, the northwest of Hubei Province, China. According to the legend, the ancient Chinese ancestor Shennong used to build a shelf there to collect herbs, so the place was named Shennongjia. Shennongjia National Park is also a world heritage site, a national nature reserve, a national geological park and a world geological park.

Shennongjia, a primitive and mysterious land, is synonymous with antiquity and mystery to lots of people. Its history, its legends, and its hitherto enigmatic natural mysteries and lush biological world

也丰富了景观风格，突出体现了东方文化追求人与自然和谐的理念。

西湖的美，在于人们对它的保护和历史与文化的传承。（除了）令人印象深刻的风景之外，西湖还具有丰富的文化传承和代代相传的神话传说。西湖拥有悠久的历史和极其重要的历史价值，作为文化圣地，西湖有三个国家重点历史古迹和文物保护单位，十个省级文物保护单位和一个市级文物保护单位。在整个景区，目前有一百多个景点向游客开放。每年有三千多万游客到杭州旅游，领略西湖之美。

湖北省神农架国家公园

神农架国家公园，是地处中国湖北省西北部神农架林区的国家公园。根据传说，中国古代先祖神农氏曾经在神农架搭建棚子、收集药材，所以此地后来被命名为神农架。神农架国家公园同时也是世界自然遗产、国家级自然保护区、国家地质公园和世界地质公园。

神农架是一片原始而神秘的土地，对很多人而言，它是古老而神秘的代名词。它的历史、它的传奇、它至今仍旧神秘莫测的自然奥

bring its irresistible charm. Its well-preserved ecology, rare and endangered species of animals and plants, beautiful natural scenery, numerous mysterious rumors and primitive folk customs have gradually solidified into people's affectionate yearning and incomparable attachment to it.

秘和繁茂的生物界共同赋予了它让人无法抗拒的魅力。保存良好的生态系统,珍稀、濒危的动植物种类,旖旎的自然风光,众多神秘的传说和原始民俗已逐渐固化为人们对它的向往和眷恋。

The scenery in the Shennongjia National Park is beautiful and charming. The ecological environment of the Shennongjia National Park has the following four characteristics:

Nature. In the Shennongjia National Park, visitors could enjoy the unique scenery formed by nature: naturally formed high mountains with dense forests and luxuriant vegetation; natural spring water, pure and sweet; primeval features full of ancient wild elegance; pure air, fresh and refreshing. This is the ideal place for people to return to the nature and enjoy the nature.

Mystery. The Shennongjia National Park is an ancient and magical place. Here is full of undecipherable natural mysteries, wonderful folklore, and primitive and dreamlike colors. As everything here is full of mystery,

神农架国家公园风景秀丽迷人,其生态环境具有以下四个特色:

天然性。在神农架国家公园,游客能够欣赏到自然天成的独特风光:天然形成的高山,其中丛林茂密、植被繁盛;天然的山泉水,清甜又甘洌;原始风貌,古朴而典雅;纯净的空气,清新而爽朗。这里是人们回归自然、享受自然的理想之所。

神秘性。神农架国家公园是古老而又神奇的所在,这里极富原始的梦幻色彩,充满了无法破解的自然奥秘和神奇的民间传说。由

the Shennongjia National Park has become a paradise for those who want to visit the strange sights and seek for ancient treasures. Among the scenic spots in the Shennongjia forest area, the Slatted Rock, named after its steep shape, is famous. The Slatted Rock is also the spot where the Wild Men often left their marks as footprints, hair and feces.

Richness. The Shennongjia National Park is rich in biological species. There are evergreen broad-leaved forest, deciduous broad-leaved forest, evergreen deciduous broad-leaved mixed forest, coniferous broad-leaved mixed forest, coniferous forest, thicket, bamboo and alpine meadow, which are the epitome of the main vegetation types in Eurasia from subtropical zone to cold temperate zone. According to incomplete statistics, there are more than 3,900 species of higher vascular plants, 1,053 species of wild animals, birds, fish and amphibians and 560 species of insects in the reserve. Among them, 78 species of animals, including golden monkeys and golden eagles, have been listed on the list of national key protected animals.

于这里的一切都充满了神秘色彩，神农架国家公园逐渐成了人们探访神奇风光和寻找古代宝藏的天堂。在神农架林区的风景名胜区中，以其陡峭的外形而得名的板壁岩很出名，在那里经常留有野人的脚印、毛发和粪便。

丰富性。神农架国家公园内，生物物种丰富。整个林区内有常绿阔叶林、落叶阔叶林、常绿落叶阔叶混交林、针叶阔叶混交林、针叶林、灌木丛、竹子和高山草甸，是欧亚大陆从亚热带到寒温带主要植被类型的缩影。据不完全统计，神农架国家公园内有高等维管植物3,900多种，野生兽类、鸟类、鱼类和两栖类动物1,053种，昆虫560种。其中，金丝猴、金雕等78种动物已经被列入国家重点保护动物名录。

Integrity. Covering an area of 3,253 square kilometers, the main attractions in Shennongjia National Nature Reserve include Golden Monkey Ridge, Slatted Rock, Xiaolong Tam, Watch Tower, Shennong Valley, Taiziya and so on. With rich and varied tourism resources, all kinds of tourism resources are interrelated with each other in Shennongjia, constituting an all-inclusive large amusement park, which could trigger people's endless interest and expand their vision.

完整性。神农架国家级自然保护区覆盖方圆3,253平方公里，主要景点有金猴岭、板壁岩、小龙潭、瞭望塔、神农谷、太子垭等。神农架林区中各类旅游资源丰富，各类游览资源相互交织，共同将林区变成了一个包罗万象的大型娱乐公园，不但能激发游客的无尽兴致，还能扩展游客的视野。

The Wudalianchi Scenic Area in Heilongjiang Province

黑龙江省五大连池风景区

The Wudalianchi Scenic Area is located in Wudalianchi City, Heihe City, Heilongjiang Province, 18 kilometers away from the city of Wudalianchi. As a national nature reserve, Wudalianchi was listed in the first batch of national key scenic spots by the State Council in 1983. In 1991, it was rated as one of the 40 best tourist attractions in China.

五大连池风景区位于黑龙江省黑河市五大连池市，距五大连池市区18公里。作为国家级自然保护区，五大连池风景区于1983年被国务院列入第一批国家重点风景名胜区。1991年被评为"中国旅游胜地四十佳"之一。

The Wudalianchi Scenic Area covers an area of 1,068 square kilometers. It is composed of new and old volcanoes, five volcanic barrier lakes, more than 60 square kilometers of "Shilong" (basalt platform) and cold springs with high value of health care. There are 14 volcanoes in Wudalianchi, which form in the shape of "#". From 1719 to 1721, 12 volcanoes erupted and the lava blocked the Baihe into five parts. These five parts are named Wudalianchi as a whole. Wudalianchi is rich in tourism resources, including green mountains, pure water, kinds of different lava and magic medicine springs. Wudalianchi has unique and pleasant scenery, and there are more than one hundred scenic spots. Therefore, Wudalianchi is called the natural volcano park of China, the volcano textbook and famous tourist resort.

There is an old legend about the spring water in Wudalianchi. In ancient times, a hunter from Orochun shot a sika deer. The wounded deer ran away with the hunter in hot pursuit. To the hunter's surprise, the wounded sika deer jumped into a spring instead of hiding among the mountains. The sika deer soaked the wound with the water in the spring. By the time the sika deer came out of the water, the blood stopped flowing. The sika deer ran into the mountains quickly. The hunter came to the spring, held some water in his hands, and took a bite. The tired feeling disappeared and he was full of energy immediately. From then on, whenever there was something wrong with the hunter, he would come to the pond to drink spring water, and he would get better immediately. So the spring water is called Holy Water from then on. Every year, people come there early to drink "zero hour water" on May 5

五大连池风景区总面积达1,068平方公里。它由新老火山、五大火山堰塞湖、60多平方公里的"石龙"（玄武岩台地）和具有较高保健价值的冷泉组成。五大连池地区共有14座火山，呈"井"字形排列。1719~1721年间，其中的12座火山喷发，熔岩堵塞白河河道，形成五个部分。这五部分整体得名五大连池。五大连池旅游资源丰富，有青山、纯净水、各种熔岩和神奇的药泉。这里风光独特，景色宜人，有100多个景点，因此被称为中国的天然火山公园、火山教科书和著名的旅游胜地。

关于五大连池的泉水，还有一个古老的传说。在遥远的古代，一位来自鄂伦春的猎人射中了一头梅花鹿，梅花鹿带伤逃跑，猎人紧追不舍。令猎人惊讶的是，受伤的梅花鹿并没有躲进深山，而是跳进了一处山泉。它在山泉中用泉水浸润了伤口，等到梅花鹿从水中出来的时候，（伤口上的）血流已经止住了。梅花鹿迅速跑进了深山。猎人来到泉边，捧起泉水喝了一口，觉得身上的疲乏顿时消失，立刻精力充沛。从那以后，猎人只要觉得身体不舒服，就来喝泉水，喝了泉水之后，他就马上感觉好多了。从那以后，这泉水就被称为"圣水"。人们在农历五月初五的

of the lunar calendar. They believe that people who drink "zero hour water" can get rid of misfortunes and diseases and live longer. Though it is a legend, the water here could actually help people keep healthy and prevent diseases to a certain extent.

时候,都会赶到这里喝"零时水",他们相信喝了"零时水"能够驱凶避疾、延年益寿。尽管这只是一个传说,但事实上五大连池的水在一定程度上确实可以帮助人们保持身体健康、预防疾病。

Exercises:

Ⅰ. Questions

1. Have you ever been to the West Lake? What's your impression of the West Lake?
2. Where is the Shennongjia National Park located?
3. Could you repeat the legend about the spring water of Wudalianchi?

Ⅱ. Group Discussion

Divide students into three groups according to their own preference to the three scenic spots in the text, and then the three groups recommend representatives to introduce the characteristics of these scenic spots.

Suggested Reading:

The Chinese National Geography was published by Foreign Language Press. As a series of magazines, it is welcomed by numerous Chinese travel enthusiasts. On April 21, 2009, the English edition of *China National Geography* was officially launched in Beijing, and it is the first Chinese geographic publication for global readers.

第二课 人文景观
Lesson 2　Humanity Landscapes

The Imperial Palace in Beijing

The Imperial Palace, known as the Forbidden City, is located in the center of Beijing. The Imperial Palace is called "the Palace Museum" at present. In the Ming and Qing dynasties, 24 emperors lived in the Imperial Palace. The entire building of the Forbidden City is resplendent and magnificent, so it is recognized as one of the five major palaces in the world (the other four are the Kremlin in Russia, the White House in the United States, the Buckingham Palace in the United Kingdom, the Palace of Versailles in France), and was listed as "World Cultural Heritage" by UNESCO in 1987.

The Imperial Palace in Beijing was built by the Ming Emperor Zhu Di and designed by Kuai Xiang. It covers an area of more than 720,000 square meters (961 meters long and 753 meters wide), with a construction area of about 150,000 square meters. It is the

北京故宫

故宫，旧称紫禁城，坐落于北京市中心，现称"故宫博物院"。明朝到清朝期间，共有24位皇帝曾居住于此。整个故宫建筑群金碧辉煌、气势恢宏，所以它与俄罗斯克里姆林宫、美国白宫、英国白金汉宫和法国凡尔赛宫并称世界五大宫殿，并被联合国教科文组织于1987年列为"世界文化遗产"。

明朝皇帝朱棣在位时，故宫开始兴建，其设计者是蒯祥。故宫占地720,000多平方米（长961米，宽753米），整体建筑面积约为150,000平方米，是超过1,000,000工人辛苦

culmination of 14 years of hard work by over 1 million workers. The entire building of the Imperial Palace is the largest and the most complete ancient architecture in China. It's said that there are 9,999 and a half houses, known as the "Sea of Palaces". The palace wall is about 3,400 meters long and the whole building is encircled by a moat of about 52 meters wide.

The architectural design of the Imperial Palace is pretty exquisite. A central axis runs through the entire Imperial Palace from the north to the south, and it is also the central axis of the city of Beijing. The three main halls, the back three palaces and the imperial garden are all located on this central axis. On both sides of the central axis, there are many symmetrically distributed palaces which are all magnificent.

The achievements of the Imperial Palace's construction are unmatched throughout the ages. Its plane and three-dimensional layout, its overall impression, as well as its grandeur, magnificence and solemn momentum, are the embodiment of outstanding ancient Chinese architectural art. It symbolizes the heritage of Chinese culture for more than 5,000 years, and it is also the manifestation and display of China's achievements in architecture more than 500 years ago.

The Great Wall

The Great Wall is a massive military defense project aiming to prevent intrusions by allies of nomadic tribes from the north of China in ancient times. The Great Wall is also known as The Wanli Great Wall, for it meanders for over ten thousand Li from Shanhaiguan Pass in Hebei Province in the east to Jiayuguan Pass in Gansu Province in the west. The

劳作14年建成的伟大成果。整个故宫建筑群是迄今为止中国现存面积最大、最完整的古建筑群，据说内建房屋9,999间半，被称为"宫殿之海"。故宫宫墙约长3,400米，建筑外还有宽约52米的护城河将整个故宫环绕其间。

故宫的建筑设计相当精妙。一条中轴线贯穿故宫南北，这条线也是北京城的中轴线。故宫的三大殿、后三宫和御花园都位于这条中轴线上。在中轴线两侧，有许多宏伟华丽的宫殿都呈对称形态分布。

故宫的建设成就，是古往今来无可比拟的。故宫的平面和立体布局，它的整体观感，以及其宏伟、磅礴、庄严的气势，都是中国古代杰出建筑艺术的体现。故宫象征着中华文化5,000多年的传承，也是中国500多年前在建筑领域所取得的成就的彰显与展示。

长城

长城是中国古代一项大规模的军事防御工程，旨在防御古代北方游牧部落的入侵。长城又称万里长城，因其东起河北省山海关，西至甘肃省嘉峪关，绵延上万里。长城不是孤立的城墙，而是以长城城墙为主，以大量的城市、地障为

Great Wall is not an isolated wall, but a defensive system with walls as the main body, and a large number of cities, barriers, as auxiliary fortifications.

Construction of the Great Wall started in the Western Zhou Dynasty, soared in the Spring and Autumn and the Warring States Period. Over these periods, the rulers of different small states gradually realized the importance of beacon towers and reinforced the construction. The beacon towers were connected with walls, and that was the earliest form of the Great Wall. The Great wall at that time was not long enough. After the State of Qin eliminated Qi, Chu, Yan, Han, Zhao and Wei and unified China, Qinshihuang, the First Emperor of Qin began to connect and repair the Great Wall. According to the records, the First Emperor of Qin recruited nearly one million people to build the Great Wall. Being short of machinery and equipment, the construction of the Great Wall relied on labor force entirely. It took more than 100 years to build this masterpiece—the Great Wall of 10,000 Li. The Ming Dynasty is the last dynasty to overhaul the Great Wall. Most of the existing walls were built in the Ming Dynasty in the 14th century. According to the State Administration of Cultural Heritage, the Ming Dynasty Wall stretches 8,851.8 kilometers.

辅的一整套防御体系。

长城的修建始于西周时期，在春秋战国时期被大力推进。在这些时期内，各个诸侯国的统治者逐渐认识到烽火台的重要性，再加固了烽火台的建设。城墙将烽火台连接起来，这就是长城的雏形。那时的长城还不够长。秦国灭掉齐、楚、燕、韩、赵、魏六国统一中国后，秦始皇（秦朝第一个皇帝）开始连接和修缮长城。据文献记载，秦始皇征召了近百万百姓修筑长城。在缺少机械设备的条件下，长城的修建只能全部依靠人力，耗时百年以上，修筑出了惊世巨作——长达万里的长城。明朝是最后一个对长城进行大规模修建的朝代。现存的大部分长城城墙都是在14世纪的明朝修建的。根据国家文物局统计，明长城全长达8,851.8公里。

As an old Chinese saying goes, "One who does not reach the Great Wall is not a true man." This means that only by overcoming difficulties can victory be achieved. The Great Wall is a great miracle created by the Chinese nation. It is not only the name card of China, but also the pride of Chinese nation.

Suzhou Classical Gardens in Jiangsu Province

Gardens in China could be divided into two types: the northern gardens and the southern gardens. The two types of gardens have different artistic characteristics: the northern gardens, also called the royal gardens, are represented by imperial palaces. They were built on the basis of natural landscape, with pavilions, terraces, buildings, and waterside pavilions scattered. The natural beauty is filled in the majestic style of the northern gardens. The southern gardens, also known as private gardens, are represented by Jiangnan residence gardens. They're a combination of private houses and gardens. They're small in size but flexible and compact in layout, so as to achieve the effect of "small for big".

The Suzhou classical gardens, commonly referred to as Suzhou Gardens, are the world cultural heritage and national 5A tourist attraction. Suzhou is known as "the city of gardens", enjoying the reputation of "Jiangnan gardens are the best in the world, and Suzhou gardens are the best in Jiangnan", as well as the reputation of "recreating the universe within a short distance".

The establishment of Suzhou classical gardens began in the Spring and Autumn Period when Gusu was made as the capital of Wu state. It was initially formed in the Five Dynasties and Ten Kingdoms, matured in the Song Dynasty, and flourished in the

中国有句俗语，"不到长城非好汉"，意思是只有克服困难才能实现胜利。长城是中华民族创造的伟大奇迹，它不仅是中国的名片，也是中华民族的骄傲。

江苏省苏州古典园林

中国的园林可以分为两类：北方园林和南方园林。两种园林在艺术特性方面各有千秋：北方园林，也被称为皇家园林，以皇家殿宇为其代表。北方园林往往顺自然之势而建，其中亭、台、楼、榭等错落分布，雄浑大气的风格中充满了自然美。南方园林，又被称为私家园林，多以江南庭院式园林为代表。南方园林多是家宅和园林的融合，园林面积小，但布局灵动小巧，以取得"以小见大"之效果。

苏州古典园林，通常简称苏州园林，是世界级文化遗产、中国国家5A级旅游景区。苏州有"园林城市"之美称，享有"江南园林甲天下，苏州园林冠江南"的盛誉，也被盛赞为"方寸间见琼宇"。

苏州古典园林始建于春秋时期吴国定都姑苏之时，在五代十国时期初步成型，于宋朝走向成熟，于明清时繁荣兴旺。

Ming and Qing dynasties.

Though the Suzhou classical gardens cover a small area, they are good reflections of using ingenious artistic techniques to decorate the limited space. In 1997, the Humble Administrator Garden, the Lingering Garden, the Master-of-nets Garden and the Huanxiu Villa in Suzhou City were inscribed on *the World Heritage List* as representatives of Chinese gardens in the name of Suzhou classical gardens. In 2000, the other five classical gardens were added into that list: the Pavilion of Surging Waves, the Lion Forest Garden, the Art Garden, the Garden of Couple's Retreat, and the Tuisi Garden.

Pingyao Ancient City in Shanxi Province

Pingyao Ancient City is located in Pingyao County, Jinzhong City, central of Shanxi Province. It is a

尽管苏州古典园林占地面积较小，但其是中国古代匠人运用精妙绝伦的手法装饰有限空间的很好的体现。1997年，苏州市内的拙政园、留园、网师园和环秀山庄四座园林以苏州古典园林之名，作为中国古典园林建筑的杰出代表被列入《世界文化遗产名录》。2000年，沧浪亭、狮子林、艺圃、耦园和退思园五座园林作为增补，也被列入《世界文化遗产名录》。

山西省平遥古城

平遥古城，位于山西省中部晋中市的平遥县内。作为著名的文

famous cultural city with a history of more than 2,700 years. Together with Langzhong in Sichuan Province, Lijiang in Yunnan Province and Shexian in Anhui Province, Pingyao Ancient City is also known as one of "the four most well-preserved ancient cities" of China. It is one of the only two ancient cities (the other is Lijiang Ancient City) in China that have successfully applied for the world cultural heritage with the whole ancient city. In 2009, it was rated as the most complete ancient county in China by the World Records Association.

Pingyao Ancient City has basically retained the original appearance in the Ming and Qing dynasties. Overlooked from above, the whole county looks like a turtle, with its head facing south and tail facing north. There are four doors facilitated separately in the east and west directions of the city, like the four limbs of the turtle. Because of these, the Pingyao Ancient City is also called the "Turtle City". In China, the tortoises, dragons, phoenixes and Kylins, are called "the four representatives of auspiciousness", and the tortoises symbolize longevity and health. The name of "Turtle City" also expresses people's hope for stability and unity of the nation, long-term peace and stability of the county, and peaceful and contented lives of the people there.

Pingyao Ancient City owns three treasures: the ancient city wall, Zhenguo Temple and Shuanglin Temple. The first treasure, the ancient city wall, refers to the wall around the Pingyao County. The wall is about 10 meters high and 6.2 kilometers long, which is the longest existing ancient wall in Shanxi Province. The old wall was renovated during the Ming and Qing

化城市，平遥古城已有2,700多年的历史，它与四川省阆中、云南省丽江、安徽省歙县并称为"中国保存最完好的四大古城"。它与丽江古城是中国仅有的两座以整座古城成功申获"世界文化遗产"的古城镇。2009年，世界纪录协会将平遥古城评选为"中国现存最完整的古代县城"。

平遥古城基本保留了明清时期的平遥县城原貌。从空中俯视，整座县城形如一只乌龟，头朝南，尾朝北。城中的东西方向有四个门，如同乌龟的四肢，因此平遥古城也被称为"龟城"。在中国，乌龟与龙、凤凰、麒麟并称为"四灵瑞"，乌龟象征着长寿和安康。将平遥古城称为"龟城"也寄托着人们对于国家安定团结、地区长治久安、人民安居乐业的希望。

平遥古城有三宝：古城墙、镇国寺和双林寺。第一宝古城墙指的是平遥县四周的城墙，高约10米，共6.2公里长，是山西省现存最长的古城墙。古城墙在明朝和清朝时期经过整修，但仍旧沿袭明朝初建时的式样。城墙四角修筑有

dynasties, but it remained the same architectural style when it was built in the early Ming Dynasty. Watch towers were built at the four corners of the city wall to check the enemy. Urns were built outside of the city as attachments to the city to strengthen the defense capability. The second treasure of Pingyao Ancient City is the Temple of Zhenguo. The Ten Thousand Buddhas in the Temple of Zhenguo has a history of more than one thousand years. The colored sculptures in the hall are made in the period of Five Dynasties and Ten Kingdoms. They are not only precious historical relics, but also rare artistic treasures. Shuanglin Temple, the third treasure of Pingyao Ancient City, is a Buddhist temple with a long history. The murals in the temple and the colored sculptures are all exquisite, but the most precious thing in the temple is the painted statues. There are more than two thousand colored sculptures built in the Yuan Dynasty to the Ming Dynasty in the hall. These colored sculptures, as precious cultural relics, are priceless treasures all around the world.

角楼，用来察看敌情；城外建有瓮，作为附城，以增强古城的防御能力。平遥古城的第二宝是镇国寺。镇国寺内的万佛殿距今已有一千多年历史，殿内的彩塑制作于五代十国时期，它们不仅是珍贵的历史文物，也是难得的艺术珍品。平遥古城的第三宝双林寺，是一座历史悠久的佛寺。寺庙中的壁画和彩塑都十分精美，但其中最珍贵的是寺庙中的彩色塑像，有两千多尊，造于元代至明代。这些彩塑作为珍贵的文物，是价值难以估量的世界瑰宝。

Exercises:

I. Questions

1. Do you know any other name of the Imperial Palace?
2. Do you know the length of the Great Wall?
3. Pingyao Ancient City has three treasures. Do you know what they are?

II. Group Discussion

Do you know why the gardens in the south look different from those in the north of China?

Suggested Reading:

Published by Sinomaps Press in 2020, *Tourist Atlas of China* is a travel guide to China. The portable book is easy to carry and rich in content, presenting the beautiful scenery of almost all parts of China. In this book, there are both comprehensive classifications and provincial classifications varied from place to place. The book not only introduces the geographical characteristics of each region, but also shows the folk customs of each region with local characteristics. Through reading this book, readers can have a basic understanding of tourism in China.

Chapter Five
第五章

饮食文化、用餐礼仪与茶文化
Culinary Culture, Dining Etiquette & Tea Culture

Introduction

There is an old Chinese saying, "Food is the number one need for people", which indicates that eating is a pretty significant thing in people's lives. As the saying goes, "There are seven basic daily necessities: firewood, rice, oil, salt, sauce, vinegar and tea". Among the seven necessities for people to maintain their lives every day, food accounts for six, which shows that people attach great importance to food. Chinese civilization has a long history. To the same way, Chinese food culture is broad and profound at present after a long term of considerable development. Starting from Chinese culinary culture, the following aspects are introduced in this chapter: the development of Chinese cuisines, eight regional cuisines of China, Chinese dining etiquette, the culture of chopsticks and tea culture.

Learning Goals

1. to be able to give a brief introduction to the development of Chinese cuisines
2. to learn the features of eight regional cuisines in China
3. to learn the differences among eight regional cuisines
4. to learn terms and expressions related to culinary culture

第一课 饮食文化
Lesson 1 Culinary Culture

The Development of Chinese Cuisine

During the Xia, Shang and Zhou dynasties, people began to eat cooked food instead of raw food. During the Spring and Autumn Period, four major cuisines as Chuan Cai, Lu Cai, Huai Yang Cai and Yue Cai emerged. Later in the Han and Tang dynasties, food materials became more abundant, and people began to eat around the table. The ancient Chinese often ate steamed food. Stir-frying is a prominent feature of Chinese cooking. Though it is very common now, it appeared later than other cooking methods in China. According to records, stir-frying appeared during the Wei, Jin and Southern and Northern dynasties. That stir-frying came about later than other cooking techniques is related to the popularity of metal cookers. Cooks need to heat oil at high temperature, which requires the usage of cooking utensils of appropriate materials. Because of the high price of bronze, stir-frying could not be possible until cheap iron pots were widely used. What's more, stir-frying requires more oil than other cooking methods. As the oil used for cooking in ancient China mainly came from animal fat, a small amount of animal oil was not enough to make stir-frying popular. Therefore, stir-frying was still the exclusive cooking method of many restaurants till the Song Dynasty. During the Yuan, Ming and Qing dynasties, the Chinese food culture gradually went mature and took shape.

中国美食的发展

从夏、商、周时期开始,人们就渐渐放弃生吃食物,转而食用熟食。春秋时期,出现了川菜、鲁菜、淮扬菜和粤菜四大菜系。之后的汉唐时期,食材更加丰富,人们开始围坐在餐桌旁吃饭。古代中国人常食蒸菜。炒是中国烹饪的一大永恒特色。虽然现在极为常见,实际上在中国却要比其他烹饪方式出现得晚。据记载,炒在魏晋南北朝时期才开始出现,其之所以比其他烹饪技术出现得晚,与金属厨具的普及有关。厨师需要高温热油,这就需要使用材质适当的炊具。当时青铜价高,只有后来当更便宜的铁质炊具被广泛使用时,炒才逐渐成为人们常用的烹饪方式。再有,与其他烹饪方法相比,炒需要使用更多的油,而中国古代烹饪用油主要来自动物油脂,少量的动物油不足以让炒菜流行起来。因此,到了宋朝,炒菜仍然是许多餐馆的专有烹饪方式。元、明、清时期,中国的饮食文化才逐渐成熟并形成体系。

If somebody wants to cook a Chinese dish with good color, fragrance and taste, he (or she) has to learn some Chinese cooking skills. Firstly, he (or she) has to pay more attention to time and temperature. Secondly, he (or she) needs to master the differences between different cooking methods, for there are numerous methods of cooking, including but not limited to boiling, braising, smoking, frying, stir-frying, baking, simmering, steaming and scalding. Thirdly, he (or she) has to learn how to use different condiments. There are mainly five flavors in Chinese food which are sour, sweet, bitter, spicy and salty. Vinegar is mainly used as sour seasoning; sugar and honey are sweet seasoning; balsam pear, chrysanthemum and some kinds of bitter Chinese medicine are bitter seasoning; chili, chinese prickly ash seeds, pepper, ginger, garlic, onion are spicy seasoning for daily use; salt and soy sauce are salty seasoning.

Eight Regional Cuisines of China

Due to China's vast geography and diverse groups, Chinese cuisine includes a variety of different flavors nowadays. Foods vary from north to south. Tastes also differ regionally because of the climatic differences. One summary of Chinese food is "sweet in the south, salty in the north". The local dishes with their own distinctiveness can be roughly divided into eight regional cuisines in China.

Shandong Cuisine, also called Lu Cai, is the most widely distributed regional cuisine, covering Shandong Province and some surrounding provinces. As one of the oldest cuisines in China, Shandong Cuisine originated in the Qi and Lu areas in the Spring and

如果某人想做一道色、香、味俱全的中国菜,他(或她)必须学习一些中国菜的烹饪技巧。首先,一定要注意做菜的时长和温度。其次,他(或她)还要掌握不同烹饪方式之间的差异,因为中国的烹饪方法众多,包括但不局限于煮、焖、熏、炸、炒、烤、煨、蒸、烫。再次,他(或她)还要学会不同调味料的使用。中华饮食有五味之说,五味指酸、甜、苦、辣、咸(注:辣其实不属于味觉)。酸味调料主要是醋;甜味调料主要是糖和蜂蜜;苦味调料主要是苦瓜、菊花或各类苦味中药;日常辣味调料主要有辣椒、花椒、胡椒、姜、大蒜、洋葱;咸味调料主要有盐和酱油。

中国八大地方菜系

中国幅员辽阔、民族众多,如今的中国菜也风味各异。中国从北到南食物差别很大。因为气候的不同,口味上也有很大的地域差异。中国食物可以概括为:"南甜、北咸"。在中国,各具特色的地方菜大致可以分为八大菜系。

山东菜又被称为鲁菜,是分布最广的地方风味菜系,遍布山东省及周边一些省份。鲁菜是中国最古老的菜系之一,它起源于春秋战国时期的齐鲁地区,源于孔子的家

Autumn Period and Warring States Period from Confucius' family banquette, and then adopted by imperial kitchen. It was formed during the Qin and Han dynasties. Since the Song Dynasty, Shandong Cuisine has become the representative of North China Cuisine. Shandong Cuisine consists of Jinan Cuisine, Jiaodong Cuisine and Confucius Cuisine. Shandong Cuisine is dominated by seafood, such as prawns, sea cucumbers, mantis shrimp, sea intestine, abalones, scallops in shell, crabs and flounder. The commonly used cooking methods in Shandong Cai are quick stir-frying, stewing and frying. Typical dishes of Shandong Cuisine are Braised Prawns, Braised Sea Intestines, Sweet and Sour Carp, Braised Sea Cucumbers with Scallion, Braised Pork Balls in Gravy Sauce, Dezhou Braised Chicken, Steamed Tofu Stuffed with Vegetables, Pork Pieces Simmered in Earthenware Jar, etc..

Sichuan Cuisine, also called Chuan Cai, is famous for its various flavors, especially for its hot and pungent flavoring. However, just being hot and spicy can not distinguish it from Hunan or Guizhou Cuisine, for the latter two are also hot and spicy. What is really special about Sichuan Cuisine is the application of Chinese prickly ash, which could leave a taste of numbness feeling on one's tongue and mouth. Besides the chili and Chinese prickly ash, some other seasoning like ginger, garlic, chili oil and fermented soybean are also widely used in Chuan Cai, which add many flavors as numbing, fragrant, spicy prominent, refreshment and denseness. There are a lot of famous dishes in Sichuan Cuisine: Yu Xiang Shredded Pork, Mapo Tofu, Boiled Fish in Spicy Water, Sauced Chicken Dices with Chili Peppers, Kung Pao Chicken and Pork Lungs in Chili

宴,后来被御厨所采用。鲁菜成型于秦汉时期。宋朝以后,鲁菜逐渐成为华北菜的代表。鲁菜分为济南菜、胶东菜和孔府菜。鲁菜以海鲜为主,如大虾、海参、皮皮虾、海肠、鲍鱼、扇贝、螃蟹、比目鱼。常用的烹调方法有快炒、炖和炸。鲁菜的特色菜有红烧大虾、红烧海肠、糖醋鲤鱼、葱烧海参、汁焖肉丸、德州扒鸡、一品豆腐、陶罐焖肉等。

四川菜,又被称为川菜,以其风味多样而闻名,尤其以其辛辣的风味而闻名。然而,只以辣为标准的话,不足以将川菜和湘菜、贵州菜区分开来,因为湘菜和贵州菜也是辣的。川菜真正的特别之处在于花椒的使用,它的麻可以在人的舌头和嘴巴上留下一种麻木的感觉。除了辣椒和花椒之外,川菜通常广泛应用姜、大蒜、辣椒油和豆豉作为调料,这给川菜增添了如麻、香、久辣、鲜、浓的风味。川菜中的名菜有很多,鱼香肉丝、麻婆豆腐、麻辣水煮鱼、辣子鸡丁、宫保鸡丁、夫妻肺片等都是川菜中的代表菜肴。

Sauce are representative dishes.

Guangdong Cuisine is also called Yue Cai or Cantonese Cuisine. Guangdong Cuisine originated in the Han Dynasty, and its cooking skills went matured in the Song Dynasty and the Tang Dynasty. Because of the prosperity of economy in the Ming and Qing dynasties, Cantonese Cuisine was greatly promoted. With its own climate characteristics and customs, Cantonese Cuisine has formed a complete cooking skill system and the unique cooking characteristics. Guangdong Cuisine consists of three local flavors: Guangzhou Cuisine, Chaozhou Cuisine and Dongjiang Cuisine, and each one of them has its own characteristics. Cantonese food has a light and refreshing taste. The commonly used cooking methods of Cantonese Cuisine are roasting, stir-frying, deep-frying, braising, stewing and steaming. Cantonese Cuisine attaches great importance to the freshness of ingredients. Cantonese specialties such as Steamed Mandarin Fish, Cantonese Roast Suckling Pig, Cantonese Sausage, Cantonese Stewed Goose, Salt Baked Chicken are very delicious.

Fujian Cuisine, also known as Min Cai, is famous for its light flavor and sour and sweet taste. Based on Fuzhou Cuisine, Fujian Cuisine originated in Fuzhou,

广东菜又被称为粤菜,起源于汉朝,在宋、唐时期其烹饪技术趋于成熟。明清时期,经济大繁荣,粤菜得到了极大发展。由于广东省的气候特点和风俗习惯,粤菜形成了自身完善的烹饪技术体系和独特的烹饪特点。粤菜有以下三个地方风味:广州菜、潮州菜和东江菜,三种地方菜各有各的特色。粤菜口味清淡、爽口,常用的烹饪方法有烤、炒、炸、焖、炖和蒸。粤菜非常重视食材的新鲜程度。特色菜如清蒸鳜鱼、粤式烤乳猪、广式香肠、广式烧鹅、盐焗鸡都非常美味。

福建菜又被称为闽菜,以菜色清淡和口味酸甜而闻名。闽菜起源于福州,在福州菜的基础上,结

and then combined with the flavors of the following five places: Eastern Fujian, Southern Fujian, Western Fujian, Northern Fujian and Puxian. Attaching great importance to the selection of fine ingredients, Fujian Cuisine cooks are especially good at cooking seafood. There is a very famous dish in Fujian Cuisine called Buddha Jumps Over the Wall or Fo Tiao Qiang. Since the Qing Dynasty, this dish has been regarded as the representative of Chinese Cuisine for its rich flavors, application of a variety of high-quality ingredients and the unique cooking method. There are many raw materials for Fo Tiao Qiang, such as chicken, duck, abalones, sea cucumbers, razor clams, ham, pork tripe, tendons, winter bamboo shoots and so on. Fo Tiao Qiang also has specific requirements for the food materials. For instance, the ham must be Jinhua ham.

Jiangsu Cuisine, also known as Su Cai or Huaiyang Cuisine, is famous for its sweet taste. Jiangsu Cuisine is mainly composed of Jinling Cuisine, Suxi Cuisine, Huaiyang Cuisine and Xuhai Cuisine. Jiangsu Cuisine attaches great importance to the selection of ingredients. Jiangsu has been called a land flowing with milk and honey since ancient times. Located in Yangtze River region, Jiangsu Province is rich in aquatic products, such as Yangcheng Lake hairy crab, water bamboo, euryale and so on. Because it is suitable for planting all year round, fresh fruit and vegetables in Jiangsu are abundant. Due to that, Jiangsu Cuisine attaches great importance to the freshness of food materials and refuses to use the food out of season. Jiangsu Cuisine often requires chefs to cut ingredients into thin threadlets. Among the famous dishes in Jiangsu Cuisine, Braised Shredded Chicken with Ham

合了闽东、闽南、闽西、闽北和莆仙五地特色。闽菜非常重视食材的选用，厨师尤其擅长做海鲜。闽菜中有一道非常有名的菜，叫作佛跳墙。自清代以来，该菜以其丰富的口味、多品种高品质的食材和独特的烹饪手法而被视为中国菜的代表。佛跳墙的原料有很多，如鸡、鸭、鲍鱼、海参、蛏子、火腿、猪肚、蹄筋儿、冬笋等等。佛跳墙对食材也有严格要求，如火腿必须是金华火腿。

江苏菜，又被称为苏菜或淮扬菜，以口味偏甜著称。苏菜主要包含金陵菜、苏锡菜、淮扬菜和徐海菜。江苏菜重视食材的选取。江苏自古以来就被称为鱼米之乡。由于地处长江流域，江苏省有丰富的水产品，如阳澄湖大闸蟹、茭白、芡实等等。由于一年四季适合栽种，江苏地区的新鲜水果和蔬菜供应非常充足，因此，苏菜十分重视食材的新鲜程度，拒绝使用反季食材。江苏菜经常要求厨师把食材切成细丝。江苏菜中的名菜：大煮干丝和文思豆腐都是体现厨师刀工的菜品。

and Dried Tofu and Wensi Tofu are both reflecting the chefs' cutting skills.

Zhejiang Cuisine, also called Zhe Cai, is famous for its refreshing fragrance. Zhejiang Cuisine consists of Hangzhou Cuisine, Ningbo Cuisine and Shaoxing Cuisine. Among them, Hangzhou Cuisine focuses on freshness and tenderness. It is neither as sweet as the dishes of Suzhou and Wuxi, nor as salty as northern dishes. Hangzhou Cuisine is characterized by its elaborate preparation and varying cooking methods, such as stir-frying, stewing, and deep-frying. Hangzhou food tastes fresh and crisp, changing with seasons. Ningbo Cuisine is a little bit salty but still delicious. Specializing in steamed, roasted and braised seafood, Ningbo Cuisine could retain the fresh taste of seafood as much as possible. Shaoxing Cuisine mainly uses fresh aquatic products and poultry as raw materials. The dishes present a unique rural flavor with sweet smell, soft taste and rich soup. These three major cuisines are famous for their unique flavors, and what they have in common is a careful selection of ingredients, an emphasis on preparation, and a unique, tender taste. The main cooking methods applied in Zhejiang Cuisine are quick-frying, stir-frying, simmering and steaming to highlight the natural flavor of food. Hangzhou Roast Chicken, Dongpo Pork, Fried Shrimps with Longjing Tea and

浙江菜又被称为浙菜，以口味淡雅著称。浙菜包括杭州菜、宁波菜和绍兴菜。其中，杭州菜看重清新鲜嫩，既不像苏州菜和无锡菜那样甜，也不像北方菜那样咸。杭州菜以精美备料及多种不同烹饪方法为特点，如炒、炖和炸，吃起来又鲜又脆，菜品随着季节变化而变化。宁波菜有些偏咸，但依旧美味。宁波菜以蒸、烤、炖海鲜为主，尽可能保留海鲜的新鲜味道。绍兴菜主要以新鲜的水产品和家禽为原材料，菜品呈现出独特的乡村风味，气味甜，口感软糯，汤汁丰富。这三大菜系都以其独特的风味而闻名，它们的共同特点是都精心挑选食材，都强调精心准备，都具有独特的鲜嫩口感。浙菜的主要烹饪手法是快炸、炒、煨、蒸，以突出食物的自然风味。杭州烧鸡、东坡肉、龙井虾仁、醋卤草鱼(俗称西湖醋鱼)、宋嫂鱼羹是浙江菜的代表菜品。

Steamed Grass Carp in Vinegar Gravy (commonly known as West Lake Fish), Songsao Shredded Fish Soup are the representatives of Zhejiang Cuisine.

Anhui Cuisine is often called Hui Cuisine for short. Anhui Cuisine originated in the Qin and Han dynasties, developed in the Tang and Song dynasties, flourished in the Ming and Qing dynasties, and reached its peak in the middle and late Qing Dynasty. Hui Cuisine emphasizes freshness in the selection of ingredients, usually using local ingredients. Anhui is rich in precious food materials, such as agaric, mushrooms, bamboo shoots, chestnuts, daylilies, etc.. These local materials can ensure the freshness and tenderness of dishes. Hui dishes are usually oily and dark in color. Compared with other major cuisines, Anhui Cuisine emphasizes tonic food and attaches great importance to the medicinal value of food. Hui chefs can adjust the cooking time and temperature according to the changes of raw materials. In addition, Hui chefs are good at various cooking methods, especially famous for braising, stewing and steaming. Typical dishes of Anhui Cuisine include Stewed Soft Shell Turtle with Ham, Braised Mandarin Fish, Bamboo Shoots Cooked with Sausage and Dried Mushrooms, Huoshan Air-dried Sheep, Hushi Yipin Pot and Li Hongzhang Hotchpotch.

Hunan Cuisine, also known as Xiang Cai, is akin to Chuan Cai for its wide application of chili. Most of people living in southwest of China like to eat spicy food for it can help to resist the wet environment there. Xiang Cai formed its cuisine system during the Han Dynasty. Hunan Cuisine consists of Xiangjiang Cuisine, Dongtinghu Cuisine and Xiangxi Cuisine.

安徽菜通常被简称为徽菜。徽菜发源于秦汉时期，发展于唐宋时期，繁盛于明清时期，于清朝中后期达到鼎盛。徽菜在食材挑选上强调新鲜，通常使用当地食材。安徽盛产珍贵食材，如木耳、蘑菇、竹笋、板栗、黄花菜等，这些当地食材能够保证菜品的鲜嫩。徽菜通常用油多，菜品颜色深，相比较其他几大菜系，徽菜更强调食补，重视食材的药用价值。徽派厨师可随时根据食材变化调整烹调时长和温度。此外，徽派厨师善于各种烹调方式，尤其以烧、炖、蒸而著名。典型的徽菜包括火腿炖甲鱼、红烧臭鳜鱼、腊肠冬菇竹笋、霍山风干羊、胡适一品锅和李鸿章大杂烩。

湖南菜也被称为湘菜，与四川菜一样，也大量使用辣椒。生活在中国西南部地区的人们大多好吃辣，主要是因为吃辣有助于抵御那里潮湿的环境。湖南菜在汉朝时就已经形成体系。湖南菜由湘江菜、洞庭湖菜和湘西菜组成。经典

Typical dishes of Hunan cuisine include Steamed Fish Head with Chopped Pepper, Dong'an Chicken, Spicy Salted Duck, Changsha Preserved Smelly Tofu, etc..

湖南菜有剁椒鱼头、东安仔鸡、酱板鸭、长沙臭豆腐等。

Exercises:

Ⅰ. Questions

1. What's your overall impression of Chinese food?
2. Among the eight regional cuisines, which is your favorite? Why?
3. If you were given the chance of learning the cooking skills of one regional cuisine, which one would you like to choose? Why?

Ⅱ. Group Discussion

Why is chili widely used in Hunan Cuisine and Sichuan Cuisine?

Suggested Reading:

Published by China Light Industry Press, *The History of Chinese Food Culture* is written by Zhao Rongguang and some other famous scholars. It joined in the National Publishing Fund project. There is a relatively complete reflection on the food culture of each ethnic group with its own characteristics in the book. From that, people can find the common cultural characteristics of the whole Chinese nation, especially the ecological view of "unity of nature and man".

第二课 用餐礼仪与茶文化
Lesson 2 Dining Etiquette and Tea Culture

Dining Etiquette

Dining etiquette refers to the common sense of etiquette on the dining table when having a meal. The dining etiquette has a long history. According to the literature records, dining etiquette has formed a set of quite perfect system as early as in the Zhou Dynasty.

China has been a land of ceremonies since ancient times. Chinese culture has a long history. Among different cultures, table culture is an important one, and dining etiquette is the main content of table culture. In China, eating plays an important role in people's lives, for eating cannot only meet people's needs, but also is an important way of social communication. Dining promotes closer and better relationships among family members, friends, relatives, co-workers and neighbors.

In China, people are not allowed to sit down at will in banquets. Chinese dining tables are generally divided into round tables and square tables. The general seating principle of round tables is right oriented and front door oriented. That is to say, the middle position facing the door is the chief's seat. The seat of the chief is the most honorable, and then it comes to the seats on the sides of the chief. The closer you are to the head, the more exalted your position is, and the farther you are from the seat of the chief, the less exalted your

用餐礼仪

用餐礼仪指的是在餐桌上的用餐过程中所体现出的通识礼仪。用餐礼仪历史悠久，根据史料记载，早在周朝时期，用餐就已经形成了一套较为完整的礼仪体系。

中国自古以来就是礼仪之邦。中国文化源远流长，其中，餐桌文化是中国文化的重要组成部分，而用餐礼仪又是餐桌文化的主要内容。在中国，吃饭在人们的生活中占据重要的地位，因为吃饭不仅仅能满足人们的正常生活需求，它也是一种重要的社会交际方式。用餐能够促使家庭成员之间、朋友亲戚之间、同事以及邻居之间形成更为亲密、良好的关系。

在中国，人们就餐时不能随意落座。中国的餐桌一般分为圆桌和方桌两种。圆桌的座位安排的总体原则是：以右为尊、以面朝正门为上，也就是说，面朝正门并且居于最中间的位置是首席。首席的座位最为尊贵，首席两旁的座位次之。距离首席越近，位置越尊贵，随着距离首席的座位变远，尊贵程度随之降低。在同等距离下，

position is. The position on the right hand side of the head is more distinguished than the position on the left at the same distance.

The general principle of seat arrangement of square tables is the same as of round tables, which is right oriented and front door oriented. Being different from long tables used abroad, the Baxian table is the top choice among those Chinese square tables in China. The Baxian table is a big square table for Chinese people to eat and drink. The table allows eight people to sit around, with two of them at one direction. If there are seats of the Baxian table facing the gate, the seat on the right side of the two seats is the chief seat. If there is no seat facing the gate, the seat on the right side of the seats facing the east is the chief.

When taking a seat, people should pay attention to the following points: 1. Guests take the seats first; 2. Elders take the seats second; 3. Ladies have the priority of taking seats after elders; 4. After taking seats, people should not put their elbows on the table and play with the cutlery, just sitting up straight and waiting for the meal; 5. When people need to leave the table first, they should signal to the host and other guests, "I am full; please enjoy the meal slowly", and then leave the table.

When invited to a dinner party, guests should pay attention to their manners before, during and after the meal. First of all, guests should be punctual and arrive at the dining place on time. After taking the seats, they should pay attention to the usage of the napkin. The function of the napkin is to prevent greasy dirt on clothes, so the guests should spread the napkin on their thighs and don't play with it at will. Secondly, guests should check whether their tableware is enough or not.

首席右手边的位置比左手边的位置更尊贵。

方桌的座位安排的总体原则同圆桌一样，也是"以右为尊、以面朝正门为上"。与国外长桌不同，中国的方桌一般以八仙桌为首选。八仙桌是中国人吃饭、饮酒用的大正方桌，可以围坐八个人，每侧坐两人。如果八仙桌有面朝大门的座位，那么两个座位中，居于右侧的座位为首席。如果没有面朝大门的座位，则面朝东方的一侧座位中，居于右侧的座位为首席。

在就座时，人们应该注意以下几点：1.客人优先入座；2.长辈随后入座；3.长辈坐定后，女士入座；4.入座后，保持坐姿端正，等待开餐不要把手肘放在桌子上，不要玩弄桌上的餐具。5.当需要先行离席时，应向主人及其他宾客示意："我吃饱了，大家请慢用"，然后再离开餐桌。

被邀请赴宴时，客人应注意自己在餐前、餐中和餐后的礼仪。首先，应注意守时，准时到达用餐地点。入座后，应注意餐巾的使用。餐巾的作用是防止油污弄脏衣服，所以应把餐巾平铺在大腿上，不能随意把玩。其次，客人应查看自己的餐具是否齐全，如缺少餐具，应及时向服务员索要。再次，要把手

If something is absent, they should ask the waiter for it in time. In addition, items such as mobile phones should be placed in carry-on bags, for it is impolite to play with mobile phones during meals.

In the process of dining, there are many things that need more carefulness. For instance: Wait for the guest or the elder to take the seat first to show respect. Pick dishes close to you. Don't lean out to pick dishes far away. Keep lips tight to avoid making loud noise when eating. Don't use somebody's own chopsticks to pick up the dishes for the guests, using public chopsticks instead. Don't rush to pick up the dishes, and don't eat one dish only. Be easy and elegant, and swallow slowly. Don't talk to others when having food in your mouth. Do not spit out the food in mouth; If the food is very hot, people could drink some ice water for relief. Do not spit bones and other things on the table or on the ground. If the table is a rotating one, pay attention not to rotate it when someone is picking up some dish at the same time. When rotating the table, follow the clockwise direction. Avoid the behavior like hiccups, sneezing and smoking. During the meal, you should not only eat from the beginning to the end of the meal, but chat with the host and guests timely to create a good and harmonious atmosphere.

After eating and drinking, the following things should be paid attention to: 1. Do not pick teeth. If it is necessary, people could pick their teeth after covering that with their hands. After picking the teeth, remove the toothpick and do not communicate with others by biting it. 2. Place the tableware neatly after finishing the meal. 3. Do not leave the seat without permission and wait for the host to signal the end of the banquet.

机等物品放置在随身携带的包内，因为吃饭时玩手机是不礼貌的行为。

在用餐的过程中，需要特别注意的事情有很多，比如：请客人或长辈先就座以示尊敬。夹取距离自己近的菜，不要探身去夹取远距离的菜品。吃饭时闭紧双唇，以免发出较大的噪声。不要用自己的筷子给客人夹菜，要使用公筷。不要抢着夹菜，也不要只吃一盘菜。从容优雅，细嚼慢咽。嘴里有食物的时候不要同他人讲话。吃进嘴的食物不可以吐出来。如果食物比较烫的话，可以喝一些冰水缓解。吃剩的骨头等物不要直接吐在桌子上或地上。如果桌子是旋转餐桌，注意有人夹菜时不要旋转餐桌，在旋转餐桌时按照顺时针方向。吃饭时，避免如打嗝、打喷嚏、抽烟的行为。吃饭时，不能从头吃到尾，要适时和主人、宾客聊天，营造良好和谐的就餐氛围。

吃饱喝足后，有以下几点要注意：1.不要剔牙。如确实有必要，可以以手遮挡。剔牙完成后，将牙签拿开，不可以咬着牙签与人交流；2.用餐结束后，将餐具摆放整齐；3.不要擅自离开座位，等待主人示意宴请结束；4.等待主人和主要宾客离席后，再离开座位；5.餐后向主

4. Keep on your seat before the leaving of the host and key guests. 5. Express thanks to the host and leave politely after the meal.

Chopsticks

Chopsticks originated in China and are the most commonly used tableware in China. There are many raw materials for making chopsticks, such as bamboo, plastic, wood, ivory, gold, silver, copper and other metals.

Chinese ancient chopsticks are round at one end and square at the other. The round end symbolizes the heaven and the square end symbolizes the earth, which corresponds to the ancient cognition of "round sky and square earth".

Using chopsticks is not only an inheritance of Chinese traditional culture, but also of great benefit to people's physical and mental development. Using chopsticks cannot only improve the dexterity of the fingers, but also enhance the ability of multiple joints and muscle units, including shoulders, arms, wrists and palms. In addition, using chopsticks can also promote visual development and mental health of people.

人表示感谢,礼貌离开。

筷子

筷子起源于中国,是中国最常用的餐具。制作筷子的原材料有很多,如竹子、塑料、木头、象牙、金、银、铜,以及其他金属。

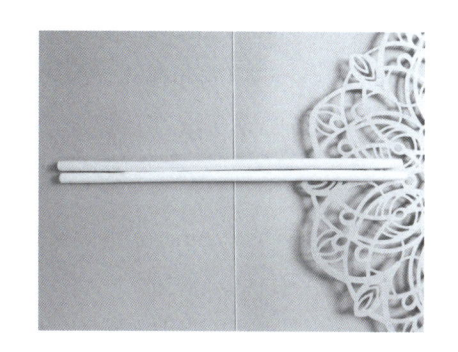

古代中国的筷子一头是圆形的,另一头是方形的。圆的一头象征天,方的一头象征地,对应"天圆地方"的古代认知。

使用筷子不仅是对中国传统文化的继承,而且对于人的身体和智力发育都有很大的好处。使用筷子不但能够锻炼人的手指的灵活度,还可以锻炼包括肩部、胳膊、手腕和手掌在内的多个关节和肌肉单位的能力。此外,使用筷子还能够促进人们的视觉发育和精神健康。

There are also some taboos of using chopsticks. For example, do not insert chopsticks directly above the food. Do not use chopsticks as knives to tear meat dishes. Do not use chopsticks as sticks to get food. Do not tap utensils and tables with chopsticks. Do not put chopsticks in your mouth and suck them. Do not point at people with chopsticks. Don't hesitate to pick up food when using chopsticks. Try not to spill the soup when clamping dish. Don't use chopsticks to poke around in the dish and so on. If you are invited to a banquet, try to avoid the above improper usage of chopsticks at the dining table.

Tea Culture

China is the home of tea, and consumes the most tea in the world currently. As the national drink of China, tea is deeply loved by the Chinese people. Chinese tea culture has a long history of thousands of years. According to legend, the first person who found the magic effect of tea is Shennong, Emperor Yan. During the Period of the Three Emperors and Five Sovereigns, Shennong tasted hundreds of herbs. On one occasion, Shennong ate a poisonous grass by mistake. As he was dying, he leaned against a tree by the roadside. At this time, a leaf from the tree suddenly fell into his mouth. Shennong chewed the leaf and swallowed it, then he found that his body recovered a lot, and most of the poison was neutralized. This leaf, with its magical effect, is tea. Since then, Shennong, relying on the detoxification effect of tea, had tasted hundreds of herbs. He also brought tea to human beings, and since then tea has begun to play an increasingly important role in people's lives.

使用筷子也有一些禁忌，比如：不能把筷子直接插在食物上方；不能把筷子作为刀子使用，撕扯肉类菜肴；不能把筷子作为签子，扎取食物；不能用筷子敲打餐具和桌子；不得把筷子放在嘴里吮吸；不得用筷子指人；用筷子夹菜时不得犹豫不决；夹菜时尽量避免汤汁洒出；不要用筷子在菜盘里翻弄菜品等等。如果你应邀就餐，在餐桌上应避免以上使用筷子的不当行为。

茶文化

中国是茶的故乡，也是当今世界上消耗茶叶最多的国家。茶叶作为中国的"国饮"，深受国人的喜爱。中国茶文化历史悠久，已经有几千年的历史。根据传说，最早发现茶叶神奇功效的是炎帝神农氏。三皇五帝时期，神农氏遍尝百草。有一次，神农氏误食一株毒草，奄奄一息之时，靠在路边的一棵树旁休息。此时，树上的一片叶子忽然掉落到他的嘴里。神农氏将叶子嚼碎后咽了下去，发现身体竟然恢复了很多，中的毒也解了大半。这种具有神奇功效的叶子就是茶叶。此后，神农氏靠着茶叶的解毒功效，尝遍了数百种草药。神农氏也将茶叶带给人们，从那以后，茶叶开始在人们的生活中发挥越来越重要的作用。

After analysis, scientists find that tea contains more than 400 components, including tea polyphenols, catechins, proteins, chlorophyll, tannins, amino acids, vitamins, etc.. According to traditional Chinese medicine, tea has eight major effects: 1. reducing blood lipid and softening blood vessels; 2. anti-inflammatory and dispelling diseases; 3. thirst quenching and diuretic; 4. moistening lung and phlegm; 5. antibacterial, antiviral; 6. decreasing internal heat, removing dryness and annoyance; 7. digesting food; 8. refreshing and reviving.

经过分析检验,科学家发现茶叶中含有茶多酚、儿茶素、蛋白质、叶绿素、单宁、氨基酸、维生素等四百多种成分。传统中医认为,茶叶具有八大主要功效:1.降低血脂,软化血管;2.消炎、祛病;3.止渴、利尿;4.润肺、化痰;5.抗菌、抗病毒;6.清热降火,祛燥祛烦;7.消食;8.提神醒脑。

Exercises:

Ⅰ. Questions

1. On Chinese dining tables, there are several commonly observed rules of etiquette. Can you list any after learning this lesson?
2. Chopsticks and spoons, which would you prefer to use? List your reasons.
3. Among green tea, black tea, yellow tea, white tea, dark tea, scented tea and oolong, which type of tea is your favorite? Why?

Ⅱ. Group Discussion

1. Are there any customs of drinking tea in your hometown? If yes, list some.
2. Could you list the advantages of using chopsticks?

Suggested Reading:

The Introduction to Chinese Food Culture is a textbook of the "12th Five-Year Plan" of higher vocational education. The first edition of this book was published in 2017 and the second edition was published in 2019 by the China Light Industry Press. The main content of the book includes: overview of the Chinese food culture; features of Chinese food culture in different historical periods; introduction of Chinese dishes and Chinese pasta; Chinese tea culture and wine culture; the diet etiquette, etc.. Researched from different aspects, this book gives a comprehensive and detailed introduction to Chinese food culture.

Chapter Six

传统服饰与艺术品
Traditional Clothing and Art Crafts

Introduction

As one of the birth places of world civilizations, China has enjoyed the high level of civilization in clothing and art crafts, which reflects the economic and cultural development in different dynasties as well as people's lives and minds in different regions. Traditional Chinese clothing and art crafts not only represent rapid changing fashion trends and people's minds, but also indicate the relationship between art and craftsmanship in different periods of a society. This chapter not only provides you with the whole history of Chinese clothing and art crafts, but also displays the distinguished features and classical artworks in typical dynasties. In terms of daily dressing and adornment, you will know about the life of common Chinese people objectively.

Learning Goals

1. to learn the representative clothing styles and art crafts in different dynasties
2. to learn the cultural codes of traditional clothing and art crafts
3. to compare Chinese clothing and art crafts with those of other countries
4. to know about Chinese bronze ware
5. to know about traditional handicrafts, paper-cutting and embroidery
6. to know about major art works of porcelain decorations

第一课 传统服饰
Lesson 1 Traditional Clothing

The Origin of Clothes

There are few Chinese unified writing records before the Qin Dynasty. Regarding the origin of clothing, ancient Chinese people have several guesses including for protection, embarrassment and decoration. According to the historic records, clothes are mainly made of animal furs sewed through bone needles with the development of history. In other words, Chinese ancient people had already learned the technology of sewing together animal skins. The earliest bone needle in China was found in Zhou Kou Dian, Beijing, dating back to around 10,000 years ago. The spicule was polished from a long and thin bone and was drilled a small hole in relatively blunt section. In the period of Yellow Emperor, there was a saying for clothing called "Shang Yi and Xia Shang". Although the clothing materials were pretty common and rough,

服饰的起源

先秦时代，少有统一的中国文字记载。关于服饰的起源，中国古人主要有如下猜想：保护、遮羞和装饰。根据历史记载，随着历史的发展，人们的衣服主要以兽皮为原材料，由骨针缝制而成。换句话说，中国古人已经掌握了将兽皮缝制到一起的技术。目前发现的最早的缝衣骨针是在北京周口店出土的，距今约有一万年的历史。骨针是将长形的细兽骨打磨成针状，并在较钝的一端钻一个小孔而成。到了黄帝时期，有了"上衣下裳"的说法。尽管衣裳的材质很普通也很粗糙，如亚麻布、天然丝织物、兽皮，甚至是树叶，古代中国人

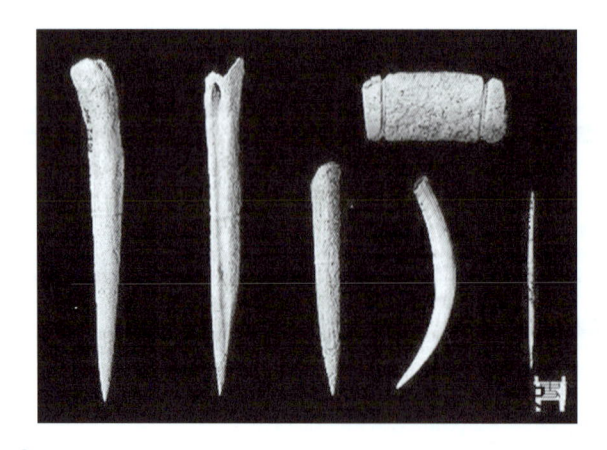

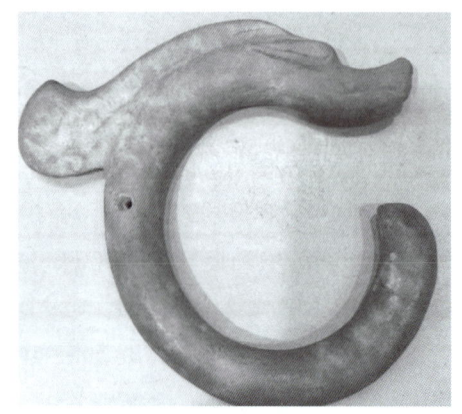

such as linen, natural silk, furs and even tree leaves, Chinese people started to make the Jade accessories on what they called "clothes". Jade is the symbol of elegance and preciousness in traditional Chinese culture. There is an old saying, "A gentleman is as gentle as a jade." The pursuit of beauty for Chinese people has never ceased since then.

Formal Dress for Civilians—Shenyi in the Chu and Han Dynasties

The essence of Han culture mainly inherited cultural characteristics from the Chu and Han dynasties, and clothing, as an important aspect of culture embodying the life and society, has always been concerned by Chinese and foreign experts. In accordance with culture, most of Chinese clothes of the Chu and Han dynasties were very long and narrow according to the lanky body of ancient Chinese. Shenyi was composed of Shang Yi and Xia Shang, and was one of the classical clothing styles in this period. It was widely accepted not only for the noble, but also for civilians.

There were two kinds of Shenyi, which were the curving-front robe and the straight-front robe. Chinese literal meaning of Shenyi is to cover the whole body in many layers of cloth. The leaders of the Han Dynasty believed the ethics of *Rites of Zhou* — the book containing rituals and rules of behaviour and garments in this period of time. Despite the set of etiquette and cultural values, people were always pursuing the innovative styles, patterns and colors of Shenyi. Special colors were used for clothing in harmony with nature and ceremonies. For example, many people preferred to wear green in spring, red in summer, yellow in autumn and black in winter. They were also required to dress in

开始用玉石饰物装饰他们所谓的"衣服"。玉在中国传统文化中代表高贵与珍稀，古有"君子温润如玉"的说法。中国人对美的追求从古至今未曾停歇。

楚汉时期的平民服装：深衣

汉文化精髓主要传承于楚汉时期的文化特色。服饰作为一种重要的社会生活文化表象，一直备受中外专家关注。与文化相一致，大多数楚汉时期的中国服饰非常长且瘦，与中国古人的瘦高身材相一致。深衣由上衣与下裳组合而成，是这个时期典型的服饰风格之一，贵族和平民普遍接受。

深衣有曲裾和直裾两款。深衣，顾名思义，是以很多层布料遮住整个身体。汉朝的领导者信奉《周礼》，这本书涵盖了当时的礼仪行为准则。尽管有礼仪和文化价值观的束缚，人们依然不断追求深衣的创新风格、样式以及颜色。服装的特定颜色与自然和典礼仪式保持和谐。比如，很多人喜欢在春季着绿色、夏季着红色、秋季着黄色、冬季着黑色。人们也会被要求在婚礼上穿代表喜庆的红色，葬礼上穿代表庄严的黑色。在当时，很

red representing joy for wedding ceremonies and black representing seriousness for funerals. At that time, ladies liked to tailor their dressings according to females' figures with fabulous waistline and colorful patterns. The varied figures of slim dancing females appeared in many art crafts and paintings.

多古代女性将深衣依据个人身材进行改良，并配以美丽的腰带和多彩的图案。各种身材纤细的女性舞者形象出现在很多艺术品和绘画中。

Military Uniforms—Liang Dang in the Wei, Jin, South and North Dynasties

魏晋南北朝时期的戎装：裲裆

The Wei, Jin, South and North dynasties were the most changing period with political chaos in Chinese history, and the political turmoil brought with frequent changes in clothing styles. As northern ethnic groups

魏晋南北朝时期是中国历史上政治最混乱多变的时期，政治上的动荡带来了服饰风格的频繁变化。随着北方少数民族入主中原，

moved and dominated the central plain of China, the fusion of culture from ethnic groups had a positive influence on the development of costume. As the long name for this period of Chinese history, China was experiencing several regimes and rife with frequent wars and conflicts. Under such a situation, the whole country attached great importance to the war equipment including iron-making tools and suits of armour clothing. The most famous one was Liang Dang, which was decorated the vest outside the gown and tied with a silk belt. It was normal to wear the vest inside the gown previously. Thus, this abnormal feature of clothing indicated the mentality of the people in the unstable society. Besides, the hair style Shi Zi Ji, literally referred to cross-shaped, was very popular among females, especially for young girls. They preferred to set hair to form a cross-shaped chignon leaving a small amount of hair on both sides, and used a hairpin to fix it.

少数民族文化的融入为服饰的发展带来了积极的影响。如同中国这个历史时期长长的名字一样,中国当时经历了几次朝代更迭,战事和冲突频发。这种形势下,整个国家对战争装备十分重视,包括铁制工具和战时服装。其中一种最知名的服饰叫裲裆,裲裆是在长袍外配以背心短衣和丝绸腰带装饰。在此之前,背心短衣通常穿在长袍内。因此,这种反常的服装特点反映出动荡社会中人们的心态。另外,十字髻,顾名思义为十字形状,在女性中非常流行,特别是在年轻女孩中备受欢迎。年轻女孩喜欢将头发做成十字形状的发髻,两侧留少量余发,再用发夹将整个发型固定住。

Glorious Ru Qun and Hu Fu in the Tang Dynasty

The Tang Dynasty is one of the prosperous dynasties in Chinese history, which is well-known for its solid national strength, advanced culture and frequent international contact. It's worth mentioning in this

唐朝华丽的襦裙与胡服

唐代是中国历史上繁荣富强的朝代之一,以国力强盛、文化发达、国际交流频繁闻名于世。唐朝时期值得一提的是多样化,它不仅

period that variety is not only for clothing, but also for politics, as well as culture exchanges. Many foreign students, diplomats, businessmen, monks and even artists visited the capital city Chang'an every year. Sorts of exotic dressing styles poured into people's lives unceasingly. As a result, the clothing style of this period was more colorful and unrestrained.

Under the plentiful life, people regarded plump figures as the beauty for ladies. Females were more open-minded and free. During the 300 years of the Tang Dynasty, clothing had undergone three stages. Initially, the style of clothing inherited the main features of Ru Qun from the Han Dynasty which had long skirts and big sleeves. In medium term, Hu Fu, which is characterized by military uniform, was particularly popular for females. In the late stage, the females of the Tang Dynasty did not have to abide by the traditional ritual of dressing, therefore the ladies' dress with plunging neckline was acceptable and popular. In general, the variety of dressing styles became the trend under a relaxing social atmosphere.

体现在服饰上，也体现在政治和文化交流方面。每年大量外国留学生、外交官、商人、僧侣甚至艺术家纷纷访问首都长安。多种异域服装风格不断地涌入人们的生活。因此，这一时期的服装风格更加丰富多彩、自由奔放。

唐朝物质生活丰富，人们认为女性以丰满为美。女性更加开放、自由。在唐朝300年的历史中，服装的演变主要经历了三个阶段。最初，唐代服装继承了汉代襦裙长裙和大袖子的主要特点。唐代中期，具有军装特点的胡服在唐朝妇女中尤其流行。唐朝后期，女性不必束缚于传统着装礼仪，因此低领口女装开始被接受并流行起来。总体来说，在宽松自由的社会氛围下，多种多样的着装风格成为潮流。

Elegant Cheongsam in the Republic of China

The main characteristic of costume in the Republic of China was the coexistence of Chinese and Western features. In this period, no matter for females and males, everyone preferred to wear long gown on any occasion. One of the well-known dress for females was Cheongsam, which borrowed the pronunciation of Cantonese. At present, cheongsam is called Qi Pao in Mandarin. The cheongsam, made by different kinds of cloth, is a kind of body-hugging long dress for females, while the corresponding clothes for males are loose Chang Shan. The origin of cheongsam is from the traditional gown in Qing Dynasty, and was gradually influenced by European fashion. It is a bold design to show the beautiful curve lines of females. This new design is welcomed by ladies dressing up with jewelry and high-heeled shoes. The beauty of oriental females is fully displayed with cheongsam.

民国时期的优雅旗袍

民国时期服饰的主要特点是中西特色并存。这一时期，无论男女，大家在任何场合都偏爱穿长袍。其中知名的女性服饰之一是旗袍，英文旗袍发音借用了广东方言的发音。现在，普通话称之为旗袍。旗袍由各种布料制成，是一种凸显女性身材线条的长裙，男性对应的服装是宽松的长衫。旗袍起源于清朝传统宫廷长袍，演变过程中受欧洲时尚的影响。它是展现女性优美身材曲线的一个大胆的设计。旗袍的这种新设计深受喜欢珠宝和高跟鞋的女性的青睐。东方女性的美感在穿着旗袍时得以完美展现。

Exercises:

Ⅰ. **Matching**

1. Shenyi	A. the Chu and Han dynasties
2. Qi Pao	B. the Tang Dynasty
3. the earliest decoration for clothing	C. Jade
4. Hu Fu	D. Cheongsam
5. Shi Zi Ji	E. the Wei, Jin, South and North dynasties

Ⅱ. **Group Discussion**

1. What is the popular clothing for females in the Tang Dynasty?
2. What is the military uniform called in the Wei, Jin, South and North dynasties?
3. Why is Cheongsam popular with Chinese ladies?
4. What kind of factors will influence people's clothing in your country?

Ⅲ. **Suggested Reading**

George Henry Mason's *The costume of China: Illustrated by Sixty Engravings with Explanations* introduces the main characteristics of Chinese clothing in different dynasties. By reading this book, readers can have a basic understanding of the main styles of traditional costume in China.

第二课 艺术品
Lesson 2 Art Crafts

Bronze Ware—Glorious Era for Emperors

In China, the usage of bronze ware has a long history. Bronze ware was created and developed during the Shang and Zhou dynasties, which are called "Bronze Era" by the Chinese. During this era, the Chinese created the glorious civilization of bronze, which is also regarded as the significant bronze culture in the world history. Large amounts of unearthed Chinese bronze ware can reflect the wisdom and perfect craftsmanship with varied usages and high level of artistic value. Only for drinking vessels, archaeologists discovered more than 20 kinds. Compared with other countries, Chinese bronze ware is mainly used as ceremonial ware carved decorative pattern and ancient writing. One of the most famous bronze ware is the big "Houmuwu Tripod", which is an ancient sacrificial utensil. The quadripod is square in shape and huge in

青铜器:帝王的辉煌时代

在中国,青铜器的使用历史悠久。商朝和周朝是中国青铜器最早被创造和发展的时代,因此被中国人称为"青铜时代"。在这个时代,中国人民创造了灿烂的青铜文明,在世界青铜文化史上也被认为占有重要位置。中国出土的大量青铜器用途广泛,具有很高的艺术价值,可以反映当时的智慧和完美的手工艺技术。仅酒器,考古学家就发现了20多种。与其他国家相比,中国青铜器的特色是以礼器为主,器具表面雕刻装饰性图样及古代文字。其中,商后母戊鼎就是最著名的青铜器代表作之一,它是一件古代祭祀用的鼎器。此鼎造型

第六章 传统服饰与艺术品　　095

size showing stability and strength. Another famous round tripod is Da Meng Tripod, which has 291 inscriptions inscribed inside. The content of the inscriptions is to exhort soldiers to refrain from drinking and remember the warnings of the previous dynasties. Tripod is regarded as the symbol of political power in ancient China. Ancient Chinese rulers preferred to build huge bronze ware to show their authorities.

Artwork of Paper-cutting—The Beautiful World from Scissors and Knives

Paper-cutting is a kind of unique folk art with nearly a thousand years' history in China. The process of skilled artisan paper-cutting is like a magic. The artisan folds a piece of red paper on his/her hands and then gently cuts it with a pair of scissors for a few times. When he/she spreads it out, a beautiful picture appears. Paper-cutting is especially popular in rural areas. In the old days, windows were mostly inlaid with white paper which was too monotonous. Then the clever hosts cut out a red doll, or cut a beautiful butterfly, and then pasted it on the window to make it a vivid picture. The picture of paper-cutting is usually stuck on windows and gates as joyful decorations which mark the cheer for traditional festivals. The patterns of paper-cutting are mainly babies, gourds and lotuses symbolizing the blessings for offspring.

Chinese Paper-cutting has two chief approaches: the scissor-cutting approach and the knife-cutting approach.

方正、体型巨大,体现了稳定和力量。另一件知名圆形鼎器是大孟鼎,鼎内部刻有291个文字,劝诫出征将士不要酗酒,记住前朝灭亡的鉴戒。鼎在中国古代是政权的象征。中国古代的统治者喜好打造巨大青铜器以彰显权威。

剪纸艺术:剪刀和刀下的美丽世界

剪纸在中国有近千年历史,它是一种独特的民间艺术。技术精湛的艺人剪纸的过程如同变魔术,艺人将一张红纸在手上左折右折,然后用剪刀轻轻地剪几下。当他/她摊开折叠的纸的时候,一幅漂亮的图画就出现了。剪纸艺术在中国乡村特别流行。旧时,人们的窗户多是用白纸糊成的,过于单调。于是聪明的主人们就剪出红色的娃娃,或者剪一只美丽的蝴蝶,贴在窗上,使其变得生动。剪纸通常被贴在门窗上,作为喜庆的装饰品,它标志着传统节日的喜庆。主要的剪纸图案包括:婴儿、葫芦、莲花,用以象征子孙满堂。

中国剪纸主要有两种工艺:剪法和刀法。

Paper-cutting artisans are mainly females. Traditionally, the important sign of female perfection is the quality of needlework and paper-cutting. Therefore, girls had to learn them at an early age in the past. Most girls started with familiar objects such as fish, insects, birds, animals, flowers, trees, pavilions and bridges, and then gradually mastered this art through imitation until they can cut new patterns spontaneously according to their own wishes. At present, paper-cutting works are more commonly used in home decoration and festival decoration.

剪纸艺人主要是女性。擅长针线活和剪纸在传统意义上是完美女性的重要标志。因此，在古代，女孩子从很小就开始学习。大多数女孩子从熟悉的鱼、虫、鸟、兽、花、树、亭、桥开始，通过模仿逐渐掌握这种艺术，直到能够按照自己的意愿自然地剪出新的图案。现在，剪纸作品更常用在家居装饰和节日装饰中。

Porcelain—Chinese Art to the World

瓷器：走向世界的中国艺术

China is the earliest country in the world where porcelain was invented and the production technology was mature. Exquisite porcelain has been exported to all over the world since the Sui and Tang dynasties. Therefore, porcelain is regarded as a shining symbol of Chinese culture. The predecessor of Chinese porcelain is "proto-celadon", which is the product of transition from pottery to porcelain ware, and it has been found all over the country. From the perspective of fetal bone, glaze and fire temperature, it had basically possessed the characteristics of early porcelain, but the processing

中国是世界上瓷器发明最早、制作技艺成熟最早的国家。精美绝伦的瓷器自隋唐时期起不断地出口到世界各地。因此，瓷器被当作中国文化的闪亮符号。中国瓷器的前身是"原始青瓷"，它是由陶器向瓷器过渡的产物，在全国都有发现。从它的胎骨、施釉和火候温度来看，已基本具备了早期瓷器的特征，但是加工还不够精细：火候控制不够成熟，产品质量还比

was not fine enough: the fire control was not mature enough, and the product quality was still relatively poor.

White porcelain appeared in the Northern and Southern dynasties, and it opened up a new situation of porcelain production. Because of white porcelain, artisans might produce colorful porcelain. During the Sui and Tang dynasties, with the unification of the country and economic prosperity, the porcelain industry entered a new era. Important kiln sites appeared near the north and south of the Yangtze River. The technology of white porcelain was quite mature. The glaze of white porcelain of the Tang Dynasty is as white as snow.

During the Yuan Dynasty, colored porcelain increased in numbers, and it thus remained as a main form of porcelain from the Yuan to the Qing Dynasty. The porcelain vessels of the Yuan Dynasty had already varied patterns of scrolls, leaves, sunflowers, peony, dragon, phoenix, flowing streams, etc.

Tang Tri-Color Glazed Pottery was prevalent in the Tang Dynasty, with three basic glaze colors: yellow, white and green. In fact, its colors were not limited into the three, but with blue, purple, red and so on. Tang Tri-Color Glazed Pottery was a kind of funerary utensil specially for the nobles in the Tang Dynasty. They can be made into animals, human figures, life utensils and so on. The famous statues are mainly made of camels, which recall the stories on the Silk Road in history.

During the Ming and Qing dynasties, porcelain production reached its peak both in quantity and in quality. With the increased demand for porcelain production, artisans increasingly came to the prosperous city Jing De Zhen. As a result, Jing De Zhen soon

较差。

南北朝时期出现了白瓷，开创了瓷器生产的崭新局面。因为有了白瓷，艺术家们才能生产彩瓷。在隋唐时期，随着国家统一和经济繁荣，瓷器业进入了一个新的时期。重要窑场出现在长江南北，白瓷生产技术相当成熟。唐代烧造的白瓷，胎釉白净似雪。

元朝时期，彩瓷数量增加，从元朝到清朝，彩瓷一直是瓷器的主要形式。元朝的瓷器已经有了卷轴、叶子、向日葵、牡丹、龙、凤、溪流等多种图案。

唐三彩盛行于唐代，以黄、白、绿为三种基本釉色。实际上，不仅局限于这三种颜色，它的色彩还有蓝、紫、红等。唐三彩在中国唐代曾是为贵族葬礼特制的一种陪葬器物，形状有动物、人像和生活用具等。知名塑像以骆驼为主，令人回忆起历史上"丝绸之路"的故事。

明清两朝，中国的瓷器生产达到鼎盛，数量和质量前所未有。随着对瓷器的需求增加，越来越多的能工巧匠来到了繁荣的景德镇。于是景德镇很快发展成为中国的

developed into the center of porcelain industry in China and became the famous porcelain capital at home and abroad. The production of blue and white porcelain, multicolored porcelain and enamel porcelain here are world- famous and have been exported to Europe, North America, Northeast Asia, West Asia, North Africa and other places.

瓷业中心，成为驰名中外的"瓷都"。这里生产出来的青花瓷、多彩瓷、珐琅彩瓷举世闻名，一直远销欧洲、北美洲、东北亚、西亚、北非和其他地区。

Embroidery—Art Under the Fingers

China was the first country in the world to plant mulberry, raise silkworms and weave the silk. With the usage of silk and the production of silk, embroidery technology gradually emerged. Embroidery is a kind of traditional handicraft art with a long history. Embroidery products, made from soft satin and colored threads, are stitched by hand, and the varied stitching methods create unique local styles. There have been four famous kinds of Chinese handmade embroideries in China. They include Shu Embroidery from Sichuan Province, Su Embroidery from Suzhou area, Xiang Embroidery from Hunan Province and Yue Embroidery from Guangdong Province. The four local embroideries borrow elements from each other, but look different.

Shu Embroidery is the general name for embroidery products centered in Sichuan Province. After the Qing

刺绣：手指下的艺术

中国是世界上最早种桑养蚕、取丝织绸的国家。随着蚕丝的使用和丝织品的生产，刺绣工艺也逐渐兴起。刺绣是一种有着悠久历史的手工艺术。绣品采用软缎和彩线手工缝制而成，不同的缝制方法创造出独特的地方风格。在中国有四大著名手工刺绣，包括四川省的蜀绣、苏州地区的苏绣、湖南省的湘绣、广东省的粤绣。四种地方刺绣相互借鉴，但看起来又各不相同。

蜀绣是以四川省为中心的刺绣品的统称。清朝以后的生产品

Dynasty, the main production of Shu Embroidery is official uniforms, gifts and embroidery screens which is called Ping in Chinese. Ping is the representative of Sichuan embroidery. The large piece of "Lotus Carp" Shu Embroidery Screen is particularly unique, with more than 100 kinds of exquisite stitches. Centered in Suzhou, Su Embroidery is the general name of embroidery products in Jiangsu Province. Su Embroidery is famous for its extremely delicate stitches. The designs are based on flowers and birds, landscapes, figures, calligraphy and various traditional themes, with more than 40 kinds of stitches. Xiang Embroidery is the general name for embroidery products centered in Hunan. The embroidery threads are as fine as silk. Xiang Embroidery is famous for rich colors. Decorated with contrast of dark and light colors, Xiang Embroidery makes good use of light and dark grey, white and black to form a three-dimensional sense. The subjects of Xiang Embroidery are lions, tigers, squirrels and etc.. Yue Embroidery is made in Guangdong Province. It is famous for complicated pattern with different kinds of threads including silk, wool, gold thread, peacock feather and horse tail. The subjects are based on birds and phoenix with local characteristics. Being different from the others, the embroiders of Yue Xiu were mostly males.

The art of embroidery is more sophisticated today. Double-sided Embroidery is one of them. The embroidery "Kittens" is one of the representative works. The embroider divided a thread of the thickness of a hair into half or a quarter of the fine thread, and hid the innumerable little threads without any trace. No matter from the front or the back, you can see the kittens'

种主要是官服、礼品和绣花条屏（中文叫作"屏"）等。"屏"是蜀绣中的代表。巨幅蜀绣屏作品《芙蓉鲤鱼》刺绣技法尤为独特，有一百种以上精巧的针法。苏绣以苏州为中心，是江苏省绣品的统称。苏绣以精巧的针法闻名。图案取材于花鸟、山水、人物、书法以及各种传统主题，针法多达四十余种。湘绣是以湖南为中心的刺绣工艺品的统称。绣线如丝细。湘绣以丰富的色彩闻名。善于运用深浅灰及黑白色，明暗对比，形成三维画般的感觉。湘绣以狮、虎、松鼠等为题材。粤绣是产于广东省的刺绣品，以用线多样（包括丝线、绒线、金线、孔雀毛和马尾）、图案复杂而著名。刺绣主题基于有地方特色的鸟和凤凰。与其他刺绣不同，粤秀的绣工多为男性。

现在的刺绣工艺更加复杂。双面绣便是其中之一。刺绣品《猫》是双面绣的代表作品之一。绣工将一根头发粗细的绣花线分成两份、四份，又将无数小线头藏得无影无踪。绣品无论从正面、反面都可以看到小猫们栩栩如生的

lovely expressions. In some amazing designs, one side displays a cat, and the other side displays a fish. Both figures are done on the two sides of a single piece of transparent fabric and both are completed at the same time.

表情。在一些令人惊奇的设计中,一面是一只猫,另一面是一条鱼。两个图案是在一块透明的织物上完成的,而且是在同一时间完成的。

Exercises:

Ⅰ. Questions

1. What does the large bronze ware symbolize in Chinese ancient time?
2. What kind of tools should you use in paper-cutting?
3. What is the most primitive porcelain called?
4. What are the major kinds of embroidery in China?

Ⅱ. Group Discussion

1. What's the main purpose of the Chinese bronze ware in ancient China?
2. What kind of approach do Chinese people use in paper-cutting?

Suggested Reading

Chinese arts and crafts enjoys a unique reputation in the history of material culture and civilization. The authors Hang Jian and Guo Qiuhui discuss the colorful history and development of distinctive Chinese crafts, including ceramics, furniture, clothing and decorative arts.

Chapter Seven
第七章

网络与现代生活
Network and Modern Life

Introduction

    The development of globalization and technology makes the relationship among people closer and closer. This kind of era revolution is also facilitated by the variety of apps used in the modern daily lives of Chinese citizens. The first lesson of this chapter focuses on an introduction of some of these commonly seen apps, such as Taobao, WeChat, Alipay, Tik Tok and so on. Through the analyses from different aspects, readers are able to have a clearer understanding of the apps' importance to Chinese people's modern lives in the current age. Meanwhile, modern lifestyles of Chinese citizens are a key ingredient to understanding Chinese culture for international friends. Therefore, the second lesson analyzes modern lives in China from different aspects, such as online shopping, high-speed rail, electronic reading, and so on. By taking a look at various lifestyles, the readers will be informed of the contemporary style in modern China in a more specific way.

Learning Goals

1. to learn the utility of apps in modern daily Chinese lives
2. to know the key features of some of the most popular apps used in China
3. to understand the advantages and disadvantages of these apps
4. to learn the forces driving the use of these apps by Chinese citizens
5. to understand the history of some modern lifestyles
6. to see how modern lifestyles reveal the changing culture
7. to examine how social pressures create new ways of lives

第一课 当代网络平台
Lesson 1 Modern Online Platforms

Taobao

Taobao.com was founded by Alibaba Group in May, 2003. Based on the criterion of honesty and trustworthiness, Taobao.com quickly became one of the best in the domestic online trading market for individuals in just half a year in the field of e-commerce. On Taobao, individuals and business sellers sell brand-new or second-hand goods for a set price or for auction. At present, a big deal of the country's delivery traffic is generated by Taobao purchases.

Despite some disadvantages of online shopping, as long as consumers carefully identify the authenticity of online items, realize the importance of rational consumption, and observe the rules and the process of online shopping, most of the potential problems can be effectively avoided.

WeChat

As an instant communication platform, WeChat has become an indispensable tool for daily communication and monetary transactions. WeChat relies on the technology of Internet to send texts,

淘宝

淘宝网于2003年5月由阿里巴巴集团创立。基于诚实守信的准则,淘宝网在短短的半年时间里就成为国内电商领域个人交易市场的佼佼者之一。淘宝网的交易形式是个人和企业卖家以定价形式售卖或者拍卖全新或二手商品。目前,全国因淘宝网的交易每天产生大量的快递业务。

尽管网络购物存在一些缺陷,只要消费者谨慎辨别网购商品的真伪,意识到理性消费的重要性,遵守网络购物的规则及流程,就可以有效避免大多数的潜在问题。

微信

作为即时通信平台,微信已经成为一种不可或缺的日常沟通和货币交易的工具。它依托互联网技术来发送文字、图片、语音、视

pictures, voice messages, videos, red envelopes and so on. This app has frequent updates, and the users can not only realize the cross-platform communication between mobile devices easily, but it also brings more convenience to people's lives through functions such as transferring funds, mobile top-up and so on.

Advantages:

1. WeChat relieves common social pressure, and messages can be sent and received without a "read" notification.

2. It is easy to use the monetary functions, such as payment, transfer, withdrawal money through WeChat app.

3. Picture and video compression technology is fully utilized to reduce data usage.

频、红包等。该应用不断更新，使用者不仅可以在移动设备之间轻松实现跨平台沟通，同时，转账汇款、交话费等功能也为使用者的生活带来了更多便捷。

优点：

1. 微信缓解了普遍存在的社交压力，收发信息时不透露信息是否已读。

2. 微信的货币交易功能便捷，例如支付、转账、提现等功能。

3. 图片和视频充分使用了压缩传输技术，节省流量。

Weibo

Weibo is a type of blog, which is actually a microblog, and it's a platform offering tons of information and increasing interactions among its users. Commuters can briefly write their "Weibo" on their daily commute. Even when there is no Internet, users can still edit posts and save them in the drafts. Additionally, for some hot issues in lives or events that cause concern in society are quickly disseminated, weibo's real-time performance and rapidity exceed a lot of other traditional media sources.

Advantages：

1. Information is transparent on Weibo, and is released and spread quickly and widely.

微博

微博是博客的一种形式，本质是一种微型博客，它是一个提供海量信息并增加使用者之间互动的平台。上班族在日常通勤的过程中可以写一条简短的微博，即使没有网络，微博用户也可以写微博存入草稿箱。而且，一些生活热点事件或者引起社会关注的事件都会在微博上迅速传播，其实时性以及快捷性超过了众多其他传统媒体资源。

优点：

1. 微博信息透明化，信息发布和传播速度快、范围广。

第七章 网络与现代生活

2. Users are able to know about friends' lives and mood states by scanning their posts.

3. Users can share their personal feelings and opinions at any time and achieve a sense of satisfaction through receiving attention quickly.

4. Users are able to obtain information related to their interests and make like-minded friends.

Alipay

Alipay was founded by Alibaba Group as an independent third-party payment platform in China, having covered over fifty countries and regions globally. Alipay, a life service platform, has hundreds of millions of users, integrating various service projects such as financial planning, social communication, charitable donations and so on. Currently, the mainly used functions inside Alipay include payment and collection, bike sharing, ticket buying, delivery and takeout service and other commonly used functions.

Payment and Collection

Payment and collection is one of the most basic functions of Alipay. Users can pay, collect money and transfer funds by scanning QR codes. With the continuous enhancement of this function of payment and collection, there are many ways to collect and pay. For instance, users can transfer funds from account to account by searching account numbers. Friends can transfer funds or receive and send red envelopes through the chat interface as well.

2. 微博用户通过阅读朋友们发布的微博，可以了解他们的生活和心情状态。

3. 微博用户可以随时分享个人感受和观点，获得被人迅速关注的满足感。

4. 微博用户可以获取自己感兴趣的信息，结识志同道合的朋友。

支付宝

支付宝是阿里巴巴集团在中国创办的一个独立的第三方支付平台，已覆盖全球五十多个国家和地区。支付宝是一个拥有亿万用户的生活服务平台，涵盖了各种服务类项目，例如理财、社交、公益捐款等。目前，支付宝的主要功能包括收付款、共享单车、买票、快递、外卖等其他常用功能。

收付款

收付款功能是支付宝的最基本功能之一，支付宝用户可以通过扫描二维码实现收付款和转账功能。随着收付款功能的不断强大，收付款的方式也有很多。例如，用户可以通过搜索账号转账，好友之间也可以通过聊天界面转账或者收发红包。

Bike Sharing

One of the very popular functions of Alipay is bike sharing. Many bike sharing companies' services are available on Alipay. Click the icon to enter Alipay's shared bike function and scan the QR code on the bike you wish to rent. After scanning the code, the automatic lock on the shared bike is unlocked. When you finish riding, you pay on the base of how many hours you have ridden the bike. You are allowed to add this feature to the home page of Alipay if it is used frequently for the sake of convenience later. Not only can bike sharing help to save time in traffic congestion, but it also offers a green method of travel.

Tik Tok

Tik Tok is an online platform for short videos open to users of all ages, having become engrained in many people's lives. Users are enabled to choose the background music they enjoy and shoot their own short videos. Based on users' taste, Tik Tok also recommends videos the users may like as well. It positions its brand with the motto "record the beauty in your life" and the users produce vivid and creative short videos in various fields, which helps to make users' recreation time more productive. This also produces entertaining and contextualized marketing and business opportunities for advertisers.

Advantages:

1. There are so many types of videos given lots of attention to on Tik Tok, ranging from traveling, dancing, cooking and so on. Those videos empower the users to learn from others' active lifestyles and develop

共享单车

支付宝里颇受欢迎的功能之一就是共享单车,很多共享单车公司的服务在支付宝里面都可以使用。点击图标进入支付宝的共享单车功能,扫描想租赁的共享单车上的二维码,扫码后即可开启共享单车的自动锁。骑行结束后,根据骑行时间来付费。如果需要经常使用此功能,可以将此功能添加到支付宝首页,方便以后使用。在交通拥堵的情况下,共享单车既有利于节省时间,又提供了一种绿色出行的方式。

抖音

抖音是一个面向全年龄段用户的短视频在线平台,已经深深扎根于许多人的生活之中。用户可以选择喜欢的背景音乐拍摄自己的短视频。抖音还会根据用户的喜好来推荐用户可能喜爱的视频。抖音以"记录美好生活"为标语形成自己的品牌定位,其用户群体在不同领域创造出生动有趣、富有创意的短视频,不仅有助于丰富用户的娱乐生活,也为广告商催生出了娱乐化、场景化的营销商机。

优点:

1. 抖音上有很多备受关注的各类视频,包括旅游、跳舞、烹饪等,使人们能够学习他人积极的生活方式以及培养不同领域里的各

different techniques in various fields, while bringing physical and mental pleasure as well as personal improvement.

2. Tik Tok provides a stage for anyone and everyone to showcase their talents. Scintillating people can acquire more viewers making use of Tik Tok than ever before. The hidden becomes seen by the public, and the world becomes richer and more colorful.

WeChat Read

Since WeChat Read was released on August 28, 2015, it has won a place for itself among all online reading apps, relying on WeChat's existing gigantic user base. With this app's own innovative product design and unique operating methods, WeChat Read finds its own promising future by perfectly marrying reading with the social features of its mother brand.

The advent of the Internet has brought a great deal of convenience, while the Internet makes individuals more independent and isolated. However, WeChat Read's hope is that people who like to read can communicate with each other and enjoy a sense of community while enjoying reading. Thus it can become an app indispensable for online reading enthusiasts.

项技能，同时愉悦身心，提升自我。

2. 抖音为每个人提供一个展示自我才能的舞台。才华横溢的人们利用抖音平台可以吸引比以往更多的观众，隐藏的事物进入大众视野，世界因此变得更加丰富多彩。

微信读书

微信读书自2015年8月28日发布以来，依靠微信庞大的用户基数，已经在移动阅读类应用中有了自己的一席之地。它凭借自己创新的产品设计与独特的运营方式，凭借阅读和其母品牌（微信）的社交属性的完美结合，找到了属于自己的光明前景。

互联网的出现带来便利的同时，也让个体更加独立，更加孤独。而微信读书则是希望爱好阅读的人们在享受阅读时能够彼此有所交流，享受集体感，从而也使得微信读书成为在线阅读爱好者们不可或缺的一款应用。

Advantages:

1. WeChat Read provides the ultimate reading experience for a reader with authentic books in a comfortable layout.

2. WeChat Read can meet the personalized expectations from individual users, such as recommending books that users may be interested in, note taking functions by underlining, personal thought recording.

3. WeChat Read utilizes WeChat's wide user base which allows users to share good books and reading comprehension with their friends.

优点：

1. 微信读书为读者带来了极致的阅读体验：图书正版，排版舒适。

2. 微信读书能满足个人用户的个性化期望，例如：推荐用户可能感兴趣的图书，下画线做笔记，记录个人感悟。

3. 微信读书利用微信广泛的用户基础，使使用者可以与微信好友分享优质图书和阅读感悟。

Exercises:

Ⅰ. Questions

1. In your opinion, which app has the greatest benefit for Chinese people, and why?
2. In your opinion, which app has the greatest benefit for foreigners, and why?

Ⅱ. Group Discussion

1. Which apps do you currently use in China and how do you use them?
2. What apps mentioned in the text would you like to recommend to your foreign friends?

Suggested Reading：

Young Chinese web-surfers are creating their own language on the Internet. With the book *Using Baidu, China's form of Google,* you can get an insider's view of the way the new wave of Chinese youth communicates in code. Author and translator Véronigue Michel guides you on a tour of the lifestyles inhabiting modern-day "tribes" on the Internet.

第二课 现代生活方式
Lesson 2 Modern Lifestyles

Online Shopping

With the growth of society, the era of online information has arrived. Online shopping, a new consumption channel for consumers, enjoys great recognition among Chinese people. Among young people, almost everyone has had the experience of online shopping. Shopping in real life tends to have limitations. In small towns, products in real stores cannot fully satisfy people's needs. However, on the various online shopping platforms, we only need to move our fingers to get a variety of goods domestically and even purchase products from abroad.

There are popular shopping sites such as Taobao, JD.com, etc., where we can register and log into the website and purchase the products we like. And we receive parcels in several days and enjoy shopping experiences indoors instead of going out. It's quite convenient, allowing us to forgo troublesome transportation time and costs.

网购

随着社会发展，网络信息时代已经到来。网购作为一种新的消费途径，深受中国人的认可。年轻人中几乎每个人都有网购经历。实体店购物往往会有局限性。在一些小城镇里，实体商店里的产品并不能完全满足人们的需求。但是，在各种在线购物平台上，我们只需动动手指，就可以买到国内各种各样的商品，甚至国外的商品。

有很多受欢迎的购物网站，例如：淘宝、京东等，在这些网站我们可以通过注册账号，登录网站，购买喜欢的商品。稍等数日便可收到快递，享受足不出户的购物体验，方便快捷，节省了交通方面的时间和金钱成本。

In general, online shopping has become one of Chinese people's favorite ways of shopping. We don't need to spend a great deal of time shopping around, and we can purchase good products at a reasonable price more quickly than ever before by item searching or price comparing on the websites.

China's High-speed Rail

Since the opening of China's first high-speed railway on December 26, 2009, China's high-speed rail network has included inter-regional express railways and inter-city railways. The high-speed railway network in China has been the longest operating high-speed rail by mileage and has achieved the largest amount of high-speed rail construction in the world.

Before high-speed rail became popular, it took a longer time for people to travel from one city to another by ordinary slow-speed trains. However, with the networking of high-speed rail gradually forming an interconnected network, large and small cities are now closely linked and the perceived distance between them is continuously narrowed. High-speed rail is more economical and convenient, thus making it the first choice of Chinese people for travelling when it comes to visiting relatives and friends, attending business trips and taking holidays.

大体上来说，网购已经成为中国人最喜欢的购物方式之一，我们不用花费大量时间去逛街购物，利用网站的商品检索和价格比较功能，我们比以往任何时候都能更迅速地购置物美价廉的商品。

中国高铁

自2009年12月26日中国第一条高铁线路开通运营以来，中国高速铁路网已经涵盖区际快速铁路和城际铁路。中国高速铁路网是世界上运营里程最长、在建规模最大的。

在高铁普及以前，人们乘坐普通低速列车从一座城市到另一座城市，需要更长的时间。但是，随着高铁网络的逐步联网成型，现在大大小小的城市被高铁紧密联系在一起，彼此之间的距离不断被拉近。高铁更经济、更便捷，已经成为中国人走亲访友、商务差旅、度假旅游的首选交通方式。

Electronic Reading

电子阅读

E-books, as a new type of books, display their content on electronic screens. E-books solve the problems of having no room for books and the higher price of paper books. Readers can purchase books through an e-book app and own a digital version which can be downloaded and read again at any time. Once released, some paper versions of books stored in the library for a long time and will be read by many people, which is likely to cause two problems: firstly, they are borrowed too many times and some are a bit worn out and may even have missing pages. Secondly, they can be very dirty with yellowing pages as time goes by. E-books can easily avoid these problems mentioned above. When you read a book you dislike, you can delete the book directly from your e-book reader, which is quite neat and brings you no burden. As to the books you like, you can add the books to Favorites and record personal reading comprehension on the screen, which is convenient and efficient.

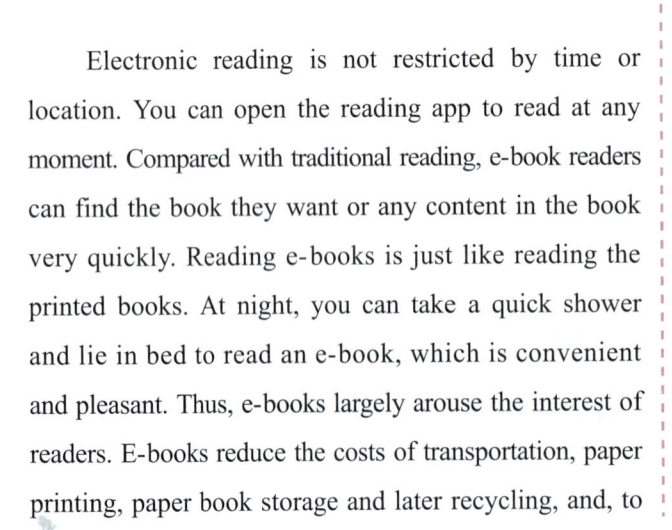

Electronic reading is not restricted by time or location. You can open the reading app to read at any moment. Compared with traditional reading, e-book readers can find the book they want or any content in the book very quickly. Reading e-books is just like reading the printed books. At night, you can take a quick shower and lie in bed to read an e-book, which is convenient and pleasant. Thus, e-books largely arouse the interest of readers. E-books reduce the costs of transportation, paper printing, paper book storage and later recycling, and, to

电子书作为一种新式的书籍，通过电子屏幕显示书籍内容。电子书解决了书籍无处存放、纸质版图书价格高昂的问题。读者可以通过电子书应用购买书籍，电子版本的书可以随时重新下载阅读。纸质版的图书一经出版，部分图书就会长久存放在图书馆之中，翻看借阅的人比较多，会出现两种问题：首先，由于借阅次数多，书籍存在损坏情况，甚至缺页；其次，随着时间推移，书页会出现变脏泛黄的情况。电子书则能轻松地避免上述问题。当读到不喜欢的书时，你可以在电子书阅读器上直接删掉，干净清爽，无负担。对于你喜欢的书，可以在屏幕上随时收藏并且记录个人阅读感悟，便捷高效。

电子阅读不受时间、空间的限制，你可以随时打开电子产品上的阅读软件进行阅读。相比传统阅读，电子书读者可以很快速地找到想看的书或者书中的任何内容。阅读电子书就像阅读纸制印刷的书一样。晚上，快速冲凉之后你可以躺在床上看电子书，方便又惬意。因此，电子书大大激发了读者的阅读兴趣。电子书减少了运输

a great extent, benefit the environmental protection.

Renting Versus Buying a House for Young People

For many young people who live in large cities for work, the experience of renting an apartment is an unavoidable experience in life.

Buying a house and renting a house are two wildly different life experiences. To those who buy a house, they want a life of more stability and hope to achieve a sense of belonging through owning their own apartments. Renters are often those focusing more on a better quality of life. For example, they prefer to rent the house close to workplaces to shorten the commuting time when their workplaces change.

For young people in first-tier cities, renting or buying a house has its own unique advantages and disadvantages. Some young people feel that renting a house is unstable and they lack a sense of security as they have to keep an eye on new places to live in as the last contract ends. Therefore, they may buy their own house through the financial support from their families together with their own savings. Some young people think that buying a house will make them a slave to the mortgage, reducing their quality of life. No matter if the young people choose to rent or buy a house, they have already displayed their own styles and never will stop pursuing their dreams.

成本、印刷成本、纸制书储藏成本和之后的回收成本，所以在很大程度上有利于环保。

年轻人租房与买房

对于很多在大城市工作的年轻人而言，在外租房是人生之路上不可避免的经历。

买房和租房其实是两种非常不同的生活体验。对于买房的人来说，他们追求一种更为稳定的生活，希望通过拥有属于自己的房子获得归属感。对于租房的人来说，他们更注重更好的生活质量，比如当工作地点发生变动时，他们更愿意选择租住在离工作地点较近的地方，以减少通勤时间。

对于一线城市的年轻人，租房还是买房有各自独特的优势和劣势。有的年轻人觉得租房不稳定、缺乏安全感，因为当他们的租房合同到期之时，又要开始找寻新的住处。因此，他们也许会依靠家庭的经济支持和自己的存款，买一套属于自己的房子。有的年轻人觉得买房会使他们沦为房贷的奴隶，降低生活质量。不管年轻人选择租房还是买房，他们已经活出了自己的风格，并永远不会停止追求梦想。

Exercises:

Ⅰ. Questions

1. What lifestyle from the text impresses you most and why?
2. Which two features of Taobao impress you most and why?

Ⅱ. Group Discussion

1. Pick one lifestyle from the text and explain how you have encountered it.
2. Which lifestyle do you think has the biggest impact on Chinese culture, and why?

Suggested Reading：

Cosmopolitan Life in Modern China tells stories of ordinary Chinese people's daily lives and displays different aspects of Chinese society. This will help readers to gain a greater and real-to-life knowledge of Chinese culture while learning Chinese. The series has 10 volumes, each of which details one aspect of China, including Chinese food, transportation, family life, education, cities and sports. There are many pictures in the series, which will help readers to gain a direct knowledge of China. The series can be used as Chinese teaching materials, or reading materials for teaching Chinese culture.

第八章
Chapter Eight

古代与现代教育
Ancient and Modern Education

Introduction

Since ancient days, China has always been attaching great importance to education. In ancient China, to be an official was the ideal for most scholars. In modern era, Chinese people pay great attention to education especially in two aspects. Firstly, the status of teachers is generally high in the whole society. Secondly, reading is emphasized in the whole society. Learning is a life-long habit for every citizen. This chapter introduces the ancient Chinese educational forms and the contemporary educational system.

Learning Goals

1. to know about Imperial Examination in ancient China
2. to know about the system of contemporary education in China

第一课 古代教育
Lesson 1 Ancient Education

Official and Private Schools

School education in ancient China could be divided into two categories according to its nature.

Official schools are the ancient government-sponsored schools at all levels which were mainly to train officials, and mostly located in the government. The official schools of each dynasty had different names. For example, the official schools in the Zhou Dynasty were called Guo Xue, Xiang Xue; in the Han Dynasty they were called Tai Xue; in the Tang Dynasty they were called Hong Wen Library and Chong Wen Library; in the Song Dynasty they were called Guozijian (the imperial college), etc..

The official schools had a strict enrollment system. The children of common families generally were not allowed to enter such schools. There were strict restrictions on admission, age and length of schooling.

Under the regulations of central government, the schooling year was varied in different dynasties. The period of schooling was six years in the Han Dynasty, nine years in the Tang Dynasty, and four years in the Ming Dynasty. All the teachers were appointed by the government.

Most of the teaching content of official schools was the Confucian classics: *Shi, Shu, Li, Yi, Chun Qiu*. Besides, *Analects of Confucius, The Classic of Filial Piety* were also compulsory for everyone. Students

官学与私学

中国古代的学校教育按其性质可以分为两类。

官学,就是古代各级官府主办的学校,主要作用是培养官吏,大多设在官府内。各个朝代的官学都有不同的名称。例如,周朝的官学称国学、乡学;汉朝的称太学;唐朝的称弘文馆、崇文馆;宋朝的称国子监,等等。

官学有严格的招生制度,平民百姓的子女一般不能入学。入学资格、年龄和修业年限都有严格限制。

由于中央政府的规定,历代官学的修业年限有所不同。汉朝时是六年,唐朝时是九年,明朝时是四年。官学的所有教师都是政府委任的。

官学的主要教学内容为儒家经典:《诗》《书》《礼》《易》《春秋》。此外,《论语》《孝经》也是人人必修。学生必须严守"师法",精通五

must strictly abide by the the regulations made by teachers. Students were awarded when they were proficient in the five classics and passed the examination.

In the Qing Dynasty, the government set up a patriarchal school (only for imperial families), such as school of Jue Luo, and school of Qi. The curriculum focused on the Imperial Examination through which students would gain the fame and career in the society. The purpose of education in school was to train the officials for the government.

In ancient China, the establishment of private schools was later than that of official schools. In the Spring and Autumn Period, Confucius held a series of private lectures. After the Han Dynasty, private education became an important section in feudal educational system, and enlightenment of education was popular in private schools. In general, there were three forms of private schools in the Qing Dynasty: The first one was "Jiao Guan". The rich people hired teachers to educate their children at home. The second was "Si Shu". Teachers set up schools in their houses. The third one was "Yi Shu". Relying on official and local public funds, Yi Shu recuited students for free. Most of the teachers of private schools were retired or non-retired officials. Private teachers offered students a lot of knowledge in the field of laws, astronomy, medicine, etc.. In a long period, the scale of private schools was much larger and more comprehensive than that of official schools. Thus private schools and official schools were complementary with each other. In general, private schools played a great role not only in Confucian classics, but also in science and technology education.

经并通过考试者会被予以奖励。

清朝时，政府在京城设宗学（仅收皇家子弟），如觉罗学和旗学。课程主要是为学生获取功名和仕途的科举考试做准备。学校教育的功能是为政府培训官员。

古代中国的私学晚于官学。春秋时期，孔子开私人讲学之风。汉朝以后，私学成为封建教育制度的重要组成部分，启蒙教育在私学中盛行。清朝的私学大体有三种形式：一是"教馆"，有钱人家聘教师在家教育子女；二是"私塾"，教师在自己家里设塾教学；三是"义塾"，义塾靠官员、地方政府出资设立，不收学费。大多数私学的教师是往任或现任官员。私学老师教授律法、天文、医学等方面的内容。在相当长的历史时期内，不论在数量上还是在（知识传授的）复杂性上，私学都比官学庞大、全面，因此形成私学、官学相互补充的格局。大体来说，私学在传授儒家经典方面和科技教育方面都发挥了很大的作用。

The Culture of Shu Yuan (Academy)

The name of Shu Yuan first appeared in the Tang Xuanzong Era. At that time, the academy was only an official collection of books and a place for private reading instead of a real educational institution.

During the Five Dynasties, due to the discord times, some feudal officials followed the value of Buddhism and they went to the scenic spots in the mountains and forests, built houses and gardens, and provided lectures. These lecture places were called "academies". Since then, the academy has had the function of school.

More than 170 academies were established in the Song Dynasty. At that time, there were four famous academies in China. Yuelu Academy was located under the Yuelu Mountain in Hunan Province; White Deer Cave Academy was located at the foot of Lushan Mountain in Jiangxi Province; Songyang Academy was located in the southern foot of Songshan in He'nan Province; Suiyang Academy (also known as Yingtian Academy) was in He'nan Province. In the Yuan Dynasty, the rulers advocated the academies. In the early Ming Dynasty, the ruling class advocated imperial examination and official schools, thus the academies could not be revitalized.

The academy had been popular for more than a thousand years since the early Song Dynasty to the late Qing Dynasty. It played an important role in the development of feudal education in China. Academies had accumulated considerable experience in the field of educational structure and teaching. It had a profound impact on ancient Chinese education for cultural heritage.

书院文化

书院这个名称最早出现在唐玄宗时代。那时，书院只是官方收藏书籍的地方和私人读书的场所，不算是真正的教育机构。

五代时期，由于时局混乱，一些封建士大夫遵循佛教的价值观，选择山林名胜之地，建造房屋花园，提供讲学。这些授课之处称为"书院"。从此，书院就有了学校的功能。

宋代一共建立书院170多所。当时有我国著名的四大书院：岳麓书院，位于湖南省岳麓山下；白鹿洞书院，位于江西省庐山脚下；嵩阳书院，位于河南省嵩山南麓；睢阳书院（也称应天书院），在河南省。在元代，书院得到了统治者的推广。明代初期，统治阶级崇尚科举和官学，书院无从发展壮大。

书院从宋初兴起到清末，盛行了一千多年，对中国封建教育的发展起到了重要的作用。在教育结构和教学内容方面，学院都积累了相当丰富的经验。书院对中国古代教育文化的传承起到了重要作用。

Compared with ordinary official and private schools, academies maintained their own characteristics in education. Firstly, students mainly chose the method of self-study, while the role of teacher was as a guidance and a supplement. Moreover, students must walk thousands of miles to meet the famous teachers. After recruitment, students developed omnivorous reading. Teachers provided students with a bibliography pointing out the order of reading, reading principles and methods, to help them to complete self-study. Secondly, teaching and academic research were combined. The academy was an educational institution developed from the collection of books. Most of the lecturers of academies were famous scholars at that time. Lecturers were dedicated to the research which promoted the teaching. This combination made a reference for later education. Thirdly, the academy allowed different opinions existing at the same time. Scholars were free to communicate with each other. For example, Zhu Xi, who presided over the teaching at White Deer Cave Academy, was an orthodox scholar focused on theory, and he invited Lu Jiuyuan from the School of Psychology to offer lectures at White Deer Cave Academy. Zhu Xi not only listened carefully, but also

与普通官学和私学相比，书院在教育上保持着自身的一些特色。首先，学生以自学为主，教师以指导、支持为辅。除此之外，学生不远千里拜访名师。入学以后，学生开展广泛阅读。教师提供给学生学习书目，指导读书的先后顺序、原则和方法，帮助学生完成自学。其次，教学和学术研究相结合。由于书院是从藏书场所发展起来的教育机构，大多数书院的讲师都是当时著名的学者。讲师致力于学术研究并以研究促进教学。这种把教学与研究结合起来的做法，为后来的教育提供了借鉴。最后，书院允许不同的观点同时存在，学者可自由交流。比如，在白鹿洞书院主持教学的朱熹是正统理学派，曾邀请心学理学派的陆九渊到白鹿洞书院讲学。朱熹不仅认真听讲，还把陆九渊所讲内容记下来，刻在石板上。这种开放式教学，有利于学术交流，并能开阔学生的学术视野。

wrote down what Lu Jiuyuan said, and engraved them on the stone slab. The open-style teaching was beneficial to academic exchange and could broaden students' academic vision.

Imperial Examination System

The Imperial Examination system was a very important examination system in ancient China. It lasted for more than 1,300 years from the Sui Dynasty to the end of the Qing Dynasty. It was the first time in Chinese history that the government used examinations to select officials.

In ancient China, before the emergence of the Imperial Examination system, the government usually selected officials by recommendation. For example, Recommendatory System in the Han Dynasty: The emperor required local officials to inspect talents within their jurisdiction and recommend the talents to the state on a regular basis. It was called "Cha Ju Zhi" in Chinese that talents were recommended to the government from bottom-up process. Shortly afterwards, the problems of Recommendatory System came up. The local officials, who were in charge of inspecting talents, were appointed by the nobility. The nobility often put pressure on local officials in the hope that their family members would be recommended.

It was very difficult for emperors to control the privilege of nobility. Even if some emperors suppressed the nobility, only few individuals could be weakened, and the established aristocratic system could not be destroyed. By passing the noble, the Imperial Examination system selected talents from the whole country directly as the supplement for the officials of government.

科举制

科举考试系统是古代中国非常重要的一项考试系统。从隋朝开始,一直到清朝末年,科举考试制度持续了1,300多年。它是中国历史上政府第一次用考试来选拔官员。

在古代中国,科举考试制度出现之前,政府一般采用推荐的形式选拔官员。比如,汉代的"察举制",皇帝要求各地行政长官考察自己辖区内的人才,再定期把人才推荐给国家。这种从底层举荐人才给朝廷的制度中文称为"察举制"。察举制施行不久,问题开始出现。因为负责考察人才的地方长官是朝廷权贵任命的,贵族阶层希望自己的家人能被推荐,经常向地方长官施压。

皇帝很难控制贵族们的这种优先举荐情况,即便有些皇帝对贵族施压,但也只能削弱个别贵族,并不能破坏其已形成的贵族体系。科举考试制度可以绕过贵族阶层,直接从整个国家选拔人才,补充进朝廷官员队伍中。

The Imperial Examination was a huge system with many tests at each level. The specific content of examination was different in each period of history. The official name of examinees would change after passing each level of the exam. If you were "Tong Sheng" and passed the three exams "Xian Test" "Fu Test" and "Yuan Test" luckily, you would become "Xiu Cai". It was the time for you to attend the three important tests "Xiang Test" "Hui Test" and "Dian Test" in the Imperial Examination. You would be the national reserve cadre when you became "Ju Ren".

The emperor was the chief examiner in "Dian Test", and examinees who passed "Dian Test" were called "Jin Shi". In this exam, all the "Jin Shi" were divided into three levels according to their rankings, which were known as "San Jia". The one who got the first place in the top level "Yi Jia" was called "Zhuang Yuan", the second place was called "Bang Yan", and the third place was called "Tan Hua". According to statistics of scholars, in the Ming and Qing dynasties, there were about 20,000 people in China who passed the exam of "Jin Shi".

The Imperial Examination was an innovation in Chinese history. It provided opportunities for civilians to be officials through national-level examination. The Imperial Examination left behind some ideas that still influence the Chinese people today.

科举考试制度是一个庞大的体系，每个级别包含很多种考试。考试的具体内容在每个历史阶段又有所不同。考生的官方称谓在每通过一个级别的考试后有所变化。如果你是童生，很幸运地通过了"县试""府试"和"院试"，你将成为"秀才"，这就是你参加科举考试中三次重要测试"乡试""会试"和"殿试"的时机了。乡试合格者被称为举人，成为"举人"后，你就是国家储备干部了。

"殿试"是由皇帝主考的，通过"殿试"的考生被称为"进士"。在这次考试中，所有"进士"按照排名分为三个等级，也称"三甲"。"一甲"中获得第一名的考生称为"状元"，第二名称为"榜眼"，第三名称为"探花"。据学者统计，在明清两朝，中国约有20,000人考取了进士。

科举考试是中国历史上的一次创新，它通过全国性考试，为普通百姓提供了入朝为官的机会。科举考试留下的一些观念，直到今天还影响着中国人。

Exercises:

Ⅰ. Questions

1. If you passed "Xian Test" "Fu Test" and "Yuan Test" in ancient China, what would you be called?
2. What are the advantages and disadvantages of the Imperial Examination in ancient China?

Ⅱ. Group Discussion

What was the significance of the Imperial Examination for the individuals and for the society?

Suggested Reading:

Education in Ancient China was written by Zhang Guangqi, published by Huang Shan Shu She Press (2013). This book outlines the general structure and development of ancient education in China both in Chinese and English versions.

第二课　现代教育
Lesson 2 Contemporary Education

Overall Requirements of Education in China

China has always attached great importance to educational development and the quality improvement of all citizens. According to *the Education Law of the People's Republic of China*, the state guarantees priority to the development of education. The whole society should concern and support education and respect teachers. The state will improve the system of modern national education, the system of lifelong education, and the level of educational modernization. Besides, the state will take measures to promote equality and balance of education. The state shall support and encourage scientific research in education in order to improve the quality of education.

The Educational System of Contemporary China

Chinese educational system includes pre-school education, primary education, secondary education and higher education. The educational system is also compromised of general education, vocational education and adult education. General education includes pre-school education, primary education, secondary education and higher education. Vocational education refers to the education that enables students to obtain the professional knowledge, skills and professional ethics which are necessary in a certain occupation. Adult education refers to the education of adults by means of

中国教育总体要求

中国历来重视教育发展和全民素质提升。根据《中华人民共和国教育法》，国家保障教育优先发展，全社会应当关心、支持教育，尊重教师。国家将提升现代国民教育体系，健全终身教育体系，提高教育现代化水平。此外，国家将采取措施推动教育公平，推动教育均衡发展，支持、鼓励教育科学研究以促进教育质量提升。

当代中国的教育体系

中国教育体系包括学前教育、初等教育、中等教育和高等教育。教育体系也由普通教育、职业教育和成人教育组成。普通教育包括学前教育、初等教育、中等教育和高等教育；职业教育是指使受教育者获得某种职业或生产劳动所需要的专业知识、技能和职业道德的教育；成人教育是指通过业余、脱产或半脱产的途径对成年人进行的教育。学前教育、初等教育、中

part time, off job or half job. Pre-school education, primary education and secondary education are generally called the basic education, among which primary and middle education is the nine-year compulsory education. As is shown in the following table: (Diagram 8.1)

等教育统称为基础教育,其中小学和初中教育是九年制义务教育。如下表所示(见表8.1):

Diagram 8.1 Educational System of China

Age	3	4	5	6	7	8	9	10	11	12	13	14	15	16	17	18	19	20	21	22	23	24	25	26	27
Academic Year				1	2	3	4	5	6	7	8	9	10	11	12	13	14	15	16	17	18	19	20	21	22
Educational Phase	Pre-school			Primary Education						Secondary Education (Middle School / High School; Secondary Vocational School)						Higher Education (Bachelor / Higher Vocational School, Vocational Bachelor)					Master			Ph.D	

Pre-school education refers to the education provided for children before primary school, and it contains family education and social education. The kindergarten is the main form. Public and private kindergartens generally recruit pre-school children who are above 3- year old. At present, there are more and more pre-kindergarten educational institutions in society.

Primary education is provided by primary schools. As part of the nine-year compulsory education, any child at the age of 6 must enroll in school. Primary education is a six- year educational system (5 years in a few regions). The courses mainly include Chinese (mandarin), mathematics, English, natural knowledge, music, art and so on.

学前教育指上小学前对儿童所进行的教育,包括家庭教育和社会教育,幼儿园教育是其主要形式。公立和私立的幼儿园一般招收3周岁以上的学龄前儿童。目前,社会上也有越来越多的幼儿园阶段前的教育机构。

小学提供初等教育,作为九年制义务教育的一部分,任何儿童都必须在满6(周)岁时报名入学。小学教育是6年制(少数地区是5年)。设置的课程主要有语文(普通话)、数学、英语、自然知识、音乐、美术等。

Secondary education is divided into three kinds which are middle school, general high school and secondary vocational school. The length of schooling for middle school and general high school is 3 years. Secondary vocational schools recruit students from middle school graduates, and the schooling year is 3 to 4 years.

Higher education is divided into two categories: general higher educational institutions and higher vocational schools. General higher institutions include specialized, undergraduate and graduate students. The length of higher vocational education is usually 3 years; the length of general undergraduate education is usually 4 years; the length of master degree is usually 2 years; and the length of doctor degree is usually 3 years. The length of schooling for a few majors has been extended.

The educational system of China has its own characteristics. Firstly, the state implements nine-year compulsory education. Parents or guardians of school-age children and relevant social organizations have the obligation to ensure that school-age children complete compulsory education in primary and middle schools. In addition, the state promotes the informatization of education, accelerates the construction of infrastructure, and promotes sharing of high-quality educational resources with information technology. In terms of foreign exchanges and cooperation, the state encourages foreign cooperation in education, supports schools and educational institutions to introduce high-quality educational resources. The state also supports conducting Chinese-foreign cooperation in running schools in accordance with the law for training international talents.

中等教育分为初中、普通高中和中等职业学校三类。初中和普通高中学制3年。中等职业学校从初中毕业生中招生，学制3~4年。

高等教育分为普通高等学校和高等职业学校两类。普通高等学校包括专科、本科和研究生。高等专科职业教育学制通常为3年；普通本科教育学制通常为4年；硕士研究生学制通常为2年；博士研究生学制通常为3年。少数专业学制有所延长。

中国的教育制度有其独特之处。首先，国家实行九年制义务教育。学龄儿童的父母或其监护人以及相关社会组织有义务确保学龄儿童完成小学和初中的义务教育。此外，国家推进教育信息化，加快信息化基础设施建设，并利用信息技术促进高质量教育资源共享。对外交流合作方面，国家鼓励开展教育对外合作，支持学校及教育机构引进高质量教育资源。国家也支持依法开展中外合作办学，培养国际化人才。

Exercises:

I. Questions

1. What is the compulsory education system in China?
2. What is the education system in China?

II. Group Discussion

What are the advantages and disadvantages of contemporary education system in China?

Suggested Reading:

History of Chinese Education was written by Sun Peiqing, published by East China Normal University Press (2009). This book outlines the general structure and development of education in China.

Chapter Nine

历史与现代国际交流
Historical and Modern International Exchanges

Introduction

China is an ancient civilization with a long history and splendid culture. Since ancient China, frequent foreign cultural exchange activities have played a key role in promoting the exchanges and mutual learning between China and other civilizations around the world. This chapter introduces the Sino-Foreign cultural exchanges in both ancient and modern times.

Learning Goals

1. to understand the historical background and significance of the three ancient Sino-Foreign cultural exchange activities
2. to understand the "Belt and Road" Initiative and its main content
3. to be able to name some of the Sino-Foreign cultural exchange activities in modern times
4. to understand the current status of modern Sino-Foreign cultural exchanges

第一课 历史文化交流
Lesson 1 Historical Cultural Exchanges

In the ancient history of China, there had been various forms of foreign exchange activities throughout the dynasties, and the most influential activities included the Zhang Qian's Mission to the Western Regions, Zheng He's Maritime Voyages, and Monk Jianzhen's Voyages to Japan.

中国古代史中各朝代都有各种形式的对外交流活动,其中最具影响力的有张骞出使西域、郑和下西洋和鉴真东渡日本。

Zhang Qian's Mission to the Western Regions

Historical Background

The term "Western Regions" originated from the *Biography of Western Regions in the Han Dynasty* written by the Eastern Han historian Ban Gu, mainly referring to the current Xinjiang region. According to this history book, there were thirty-six countries in the Western Regions at that time, but the population of each country was generally small. In the west of these small countries and the north of the Western Han Dynasty, there was a strong nomadic people, known as "Xiongnus" in history. They were brave and warlike, and were called "the nation on horseback". During the Chu-Han War, the leader of Xiongnus, Chanyu Modu, took advantage of the opportunity to expand his power, conquered the surrounding countries and tribes, enslaved and exploited them. At the same time, the aristocracy of Xiongnus often led troops south, attacking and harassing the residents of the Western Han Dynasty, trying to invade the territory of the

张骞出使西域
历史背景

"西域"最早出自东汉史学家班固所著的《汉书·西域传》,主要指现在的新疆地区。据该史书记载,当时的西域包括三十六个国家,但人口规模普遍较小。在这些国家的西边和西汉的北边存在一个强大的游牧民族,史称"匈奴"。匈奴人骁勇善战,被称为"马背上的民族"。楚汉战争时期,匈奴人的首领,冒顿单于,借机扩张势力,通过武力征服了周边的一些国家和部落,并对其进行奴役和剥削。同时,匈奴贵族还经常率兵南下,攻击和骚扰西汉居民,试图侵吞西汉的领土。面对匈奴的强大威胁,汉朝初期的历代皇帝都只能采取和亲政策求取和平。但随着国力的不断增强,西汉开始抗击匈奴,

Western Han Dynasty. Facing the powerful threat of the Xiongnus, the emperors of the early Han Dynasty could only make peace through marriages. However, as the national power continued to increase, the Western Han Dynasty began to fight against the Xiongnus, and the most famous Emperor was the Emperor Wu of the Han Dynasty. Relying on the strong economic and military strength of the Western Han Dynasty at that time, and by virtue of his personal political and military skills, Emperor Wu of the Han Dynasty finally successfully defeated the Xiongnus and lifted the threat from the north.

Process of the Mission

In 138 BC, in order to unite the Rouzhi to fight against the Xiongnus together, Emperor Wu of the Han Dynasty recruited Zhang Qian as an emissary and sent missions to the Western Regions. The first trip was from Chang'an. Since the Hexi Corridor was controlled by Xiongnus at the time, Zhang Qian and his delegation were unfortunately captured by the cavalry of Xiongnus. Subsequently, Zhang Qian and his followers stayed as captives in the King's Court of Xiongnus for ten years. However, Zhang Qian did not forget his mission, so he took the opportunity to escape and

其中最著名的是汉武帝。汉武帝依托当时西汉强盛的经济和军事实力,凭借个人的政治和军事才能,最终成功击败匈奴,解除了北方的威胁。

出使经历

公元前138年,为联合大月氏共同抗击匈奴,汉武帝招募张骞为使者,出使西域。首次西行从长安出发,由于河西走廊当时为匈奴控制区,张骞及使团不幸被匈奴骑兵抓获。随后,张骞等人作为俘虏在匈奴王庭滞留了十年。然而,张骞并未忘记其使命,趁机逃走,继续前往西域。最终,张骞抵达大月氏,但未能成功与其结盟。后来,张骞启程返回长安,但在返程途中

continued to the Western Regions. Eventually, Zhang Qian arrived at Rouzhi, but failed to reach an alliance with them. Later, Zhang Qian returned to Chang'an, but was captured by the Xiongnus again and detained for one year on the way back. It was not until 126 BC that Zhang Qian finally returned to Chang'an.

In 119 BC, Zhang Qian went to the Western Regions for the second time. Since the Han Dynasty at that time had already controlled the Hexi Corridor area by fighting against the Xiongnus, the trip was relatively smooth and the friendly exchanges with the countries of the Western Regions were strengthened. In 115 BC, Zhang Qian returned from the Western Regions and died in the following year.

The Significance of the Mission

Zhang Qian's mission to the Western Regions has great historic significance. First of all, Zhang Qian obtained a lot of valuable information about the countries of the Western Regions, and at the same time spread the national authority of the Western Han to the Western Regions. Secondly, Zhang Qian opened up an important channel connecting the Central Plains and the Western Regions, that is, the later "Silk Road", which provided a transportation foundation for the mutual exchanges of world civilizations. Finally, after Zhang Qian sent his mission to the Western Regions, the political, economic, and cultural ties between the Central Plains and the Western Regions became increasingly close.

又不幸被匈奴抓获并扣留一年。直到公元前126年，张骞才最终返回长安。

公元前119年，张骞第二次前往西域。由于当时的汉朝已经通过抗击匈奴控制了河西走廊地区，因此此次行程相对顺利，并且加强了与西域诸国的友好往来。公元前115年，张骞（从西域）返回，并于次年去世。

出使的重要性

张骞出使西域具有重大的历史意义。首先，张骞获取了大量关于西域各国的珍贵资料，同时向西域传播了西汉的国威。其次，张骞开辟出了一条连接中原与西域地区的重要通道，即后来的"丝绸之路"，为世界文明的相互交流提供了交通基础。最后，张骞出使西域后，中原同西域之间的政治、经济和文化联系日益密切。

Zheng He's Maritime Voyages

Zheng He's Maritime Voyages were maritime diplomatic activities carried out by the Chinese navigator Zheng He in the Ming Dynasty in the early fifteenth century, with seven missions within twenty-eight years.

In 1405, dispatched by the emperor Ming Cheng Zu, Zheng He led the fleet to the Western Ocean for the first time. Accompanied by sailors, interpreters, doctors and escort soldiers, there were more than 27,800 people in the fleet. This maiden voyage went from the Liujia River in Suzhou, went south along the Fujian waters, and then sailed from Fujian's Wuhumen. Then Zheng He's fleet traveled west through the Nanyang (an old name for southeast Asia) Islands such as Zhancheng (now southern Vietnam), Java, Old Port, Sumatra (now Indonesia) to Guli (now the southern tip of the Indian Peninsula) and Ceylon (now Sri Lanka), and returned to China in 1407. Subsequently, six large-scale voyages to the west were carried out one after another, reaching Mogadishu as far as the African shore. During the seven voyages, Zheng He led the fleet and visited more than 30 countries and even reached East Africa and the Red Sea furthest.

郑和下西洋

郑和下西洋是中国明代航海家郑和在十五世纪初期进行的海上外交活动，二十八年间共出使七次。

1405年，郑和奉明成祖之命，率领船队第一次出使西洋。随行的有水手、翻译、医生和护船的士兵，共两万七千八百多人。首航从苏州刘家河出发，沿福建海域南下，再从福建五虎门扬帆启航。船队经占城(今越南南部)、爪哇、旧港、苏门答腊(今印度尼西亚)等南洋(东南亚旧称)群岛，西行至古里(今印度半岛南端)和锡兰(今斯里兰卡)返航，于1407年返回中国。随后，郑和又相继进行了六次大规模的下西洋航行，最远到达非洲海岸的摩加迪沙。在七次航行中，郑和率领船队，拜访了三十多个国家，最远甚至到达东非和红海。

Zheng He's Maritime Voyages have made China's trade with Asian and African countries more frequent, and have increased the mutual understanding of customs, society, and national conditions of various countries. Messengers, kings, princesses, and officials from many countries in Nanyang visited China for trade. In addition, the voyage to the Western Ocean further promoted the migration of overseas Chinese to Nanyang. They brought advanced production technology and promoted the social and economic development of the Nanyang region. The huge scale of overseas trade has also stimulated the development of domestic traditional handicrafts, such as silk and porcelain.

Monk Jian Zhen's Voyages to Japan

Monk Jian Zhen

Jian Zhen's original surname is Chunyu. He was from Yangzhou Jiangyang County (now Yangzhou, Jiangsu), and was ordained at Daming Temple in Yangzhou at the age of 14. Jian Zhen was good at learning and once went to Chang'an and Luoyang to seek the instruction of famous teachers. After returning to Yangzhou, he had become a monk with profound accomplishments, especially in Buddhism ordination, respected as a "master of ordination".

郑和下西洋,使中国同亚、非各国之间的贸易往来更加频繁,增进了各国之间风俗、社会和民情的相互了解。南洋许多国家的使者、国王、公主和官员纷纷到中国进行访问和贸易。此外,郑和下西洋进一步推动了中国人向南洋的迁徙,他们带去了先进的生产技术,促进了南洋地区社会和经济的发展。海外贸易的巨大规模也相应地刺激了国内传统手工业,如丝绸和瓷器的发展。

鉴真东渡日本

鉴真和尚

鉴真原姓淳于,扬州江阳县(今江苏扬州)人,14岁出家于扬州大明寺。鉴真善于学习,曾前往长安和洛阳寻求名师教导。回扬州后,已经成为造诣深厚的高僧,尤其在佛教戒律方面有很高成就,被尊称为"授戒大师"。

Arduous Voyages to Japan

In 742 AD, Jian Zhen accepted the invitation of Japanese monks and took his disciples to Japan for the ordination in the following year. However, in the next ten years, Jian Zhen and his followers went through all kinds of hardships and setbacks, and all five trips ended in failure. Moreover, after the failure of the fifth east crossing, Jian Zhen was blinded due to overwork. However, Jian Zhen still adhered to the east crossing, and finally arrived in Japan when he crossed the sea for the sixth time in 753 AD.

Jian Zhen's Arrival and Experiences in Japan

After Jian Zhen arrived in Japan, he was ceremoniously treated by the emperor and high-ranking officials. Afterwards, Jian Zhen and his entourage arrived in Nara to lead the Japanese Buddhist affairs together with another local monk. In 758 AD, Jian Zhen and his disciples designed and built the Toshodaiji Monastery in Nara, Japan, which was regarded by the Japanese monks and Buddhists at that time as the highest school and holy place in the Japanese Buddhist world. Today, Toshodaiji Monastery is a world heritage site in Japan and a model of Japanese architecture in the Tang Dynasty. In 763 AD, Jian Zhen passed away in the Toshodaiji Monastery.

The Significance of Jian Zhen's Voyages to Japan

Jian Zhen's voyages to Japan not only created the Buddhist Ritsu of Japan, but also spread the cultural, artistic and technological achievements of literature, architecture and traditional Chinese medicine in the Tang Dynasty to Japan. Jian Zhen made outstanding

艰险的赴日航行

公元742年,鉴真接受日本僧人邀请,于次年带上他的弟子启程赴日弘法授戒。然而,在接下来的十年中,鉴真一行历尽艰险和挫折,五次东渡均以失败告终。而且,在第五次东渡失败后,鉴真因过度劳累,不幸双目失明。但鉴真仍然坚持东渡传法,并最终在公元753年第六次渡海时成功抵达日本。

鉴真抵达日本及在日经历

鉴真到达日本后,受到了日本天皇和重臣的礼遇。随后,鉴真一行抵达奈良,同另一位本土高僧一起统领日本佛教事务。公元758年,鉴真及其弟子在日本奈良设计并建造了唐招提寺,被当时的日本僧人和佛教徒视为日本佛教界的最高学府和圣地。如今,唐招提寺是日本的一处世界遗产,也是日本唐代建筑的典范。公元763年,鉴真圆寂于唐招提寺。

鉴真东渡日本的历史意义

鉴真东渡日本,不仅开创了日本的佛教律宗,还将唐朝的文学、建筑及中药等文化、艺术和科技成果传播到了日本。鉴真为东亚地区佛教的发展和壮大做出了杰出

contributions to the development and growth of Buddhism in East Asia, strengthened the cultural ties between China and Japan, and promoted cultural exchanges between these two countries.

贡献,加强了中日两国之间的文化联系,促进了两国之间的文化交流。

Exercises:

Ⅰ. Questions

1. What difficulties did Zhang Qian encounter during his mission to the Western Regions?
2. What is the historic significance of Zheng He's Maritime Voyages?
3. What contributions did Jian Zhen make?

Ⅱ. Group Discussion

1. In your opinion, Zhang Qian, Zheng He and Jian Zhen, who encountered the most difficulties during the voyages?
2. In addition to the three historical events in the text, what other stories do you know about ancient China's foreign exchanges?

Suggested Reading:

The Wonderland of Zhang Qian was written by Edvard Retvelatze and published by the Lijiang Publishing Limited (2017). This book is equipped with a large number of illustrations, showing the murals, Buddha statues and jewels from archaeology, which has a breakthrough academic value for the study of the history and civilization of the ancient Silk Road.

第二课 现代文化交流
Lesson 2 Modern Cultural Exchanges

The "Belt and Road" Initiative

The "Belt and Road" is the abbreviation of the joint construction of the "Silk Road Economic Belt" and the "21st Century Maritime Silk Road" Initiative proposed by the leader of China in 2013. It aims to strengthen the integration of regional economic cooperation through the two ancient Silk Road trade routes, land and maritime, to create a community of shared interests and promote world trade and economic growth. The "Silk Road Economic Belt" refers to a transcontinental channel between China and the European continent, which passes through Southeast Asia, South Asia, Central Asia and other regions, and closely connects the entire Eurasian continent; the "21st Century Maritime Silk Road" is a maritime trade route starting from China, ending in Europe, and passing through Southeast Asia, South Asia, the Middle East and East Africa. From ancient times to the present, these two ancient trade channels have made significant contributions to the development of the world economy and trade. Now, driven by the "Belt and Road" Initiative, they have renewed their vitality and become a strong driving force for the promotion of world economic integration.

"一带一路"倡议

"一带一路"是中国国家领导人于2013年提出的共同建设"丝绸之路经济带"和"21世纪海上丝绸之路"倡议的简称,旨在通过陆路和海上两条古丝绸之路的贸易通道,加强区域经济合作一体化,打造利益共同体,促进世界贸易和经济的增长。其中,"丝绸之路经济带"是指中国与欧洲大陆之间的一条跨大陆通道,该通道途经东南亚、南亚、中亚等地区,将整个亚欧大陆紧密地连接在一起;"21世纪海上丝绸之路"是一条从中国出发,以欧洲为终点,途经东南亚、南亚、中东地区和东非的海上贸易之路。从古至今,这两条古老的贸易通道为世界经济贸易的发展做出了重大贡献。如今,在"一带一路"倡议的驱动下,它们重新焕发出活力,成为促进世界经济一体化的强劲动力。

The Ancient Silk Road

The Silk Road originated from an overland trade route connecting ancient China with Africa and Europe. The main role of this route in ancient times was to transport Chinese silk to the West, hence it was named "Silk Road". Broadly speaking, the Silk Road can be divided into the Land Silk Road and the Maritime Silk Road.

The Land Silk Road originated from a land passage opened by Zhang Qian when he led missions to the Western Regions during the Western Han Dynasty. This road became the main transportation route between ancient China and Western countries for trade exchanges, and made great contributions to the exchanges of Chinese and Western civilizations.

The Maritime Silk Road originated in the Qin and Han dynasties and was the main maritime passage between ancient China and foreign countries in transportation, trade and cultural exchanges. The route departs from coastal cities in southeast China, passes through the South Pacific and Arabian Sea, and reaches the east coast of Africa.

Countries Along the "Belt and Road"

The "Belt and Road" Initiative adheres to the principle of open cooperation and co-construction. The scope of the "Belt and Road" cooperation is not limited to countries along the ancient Silk Road. All countries and regions and organizations in the world can participate in cooperation and co-construction. By the end of January 2021, China has signed 205 cooperation documents for jointly building the "Belt and Road" with 171 countries and international organizations.

古丝绸之路

丝绸之路起源于一条连接古代中国与非洲和欧洲的陆上贸易路线。由于该路线在古代的主要作用是将中国的丝绸运往西方，因此得名"丝绸之路"。从广义上来说，丝绸之路可以分为陆上丝绸之路和海上丝绸之路。

陆上丝绸之路起源于西汉时期张骞出使西域时所开辟的一条陆上通道。该道路成为古代中国与西方各国进行贸易往来的主要交通线路，为中西方文明的交流做出了巨大贡献。

海上丝绸之路起源于秦汉时期，是古代中国与外国之间交通、贸易和文化往来的主要海上通道。该路线从中国东南沿海城市出发，经过南太平洋和阿拉伯海，一直到达非洲东海岸。

"一带一路"沿线国家

"一带一路"倡议坚持开放合作和共建的原则，"一带一路"合作的范围不局限于古丝绸之路沿线国家，世界上所有的国家、地区和组织都能参与合作共建。截至2021年1月底，中国已经与171个国家和国际组织签署了205份共建"一带一路"的合作文件。

Influence and Opportunity

The continuous expansion of the scope of the "Belt and Road" cooperation and cooperation areas have brought new development opportunities to countries and organizations along the "Belt and Road" and other regions, and have had an important impact on the sustainable development of the global economy.

Firstly, the "Belt and Road" has spawned a new multilateral international development model, built a high-quality platform for transnational cooperation, and laid a foundation for cooperation to promote the stable development of the world economy.

Secondly, most of the countries along the "Belt and Road" are mainly emerging economies and developing countries, which not only adds new impetus to "South-South cooperation", but also promotes balanced and sustainable development around the world.

Finally, the process of co-construction of the "Belt and Road" has also promoted the in-depth exchanges and dissemination of cultures of various countries and has broken cultural barriers to further economic and trade cooperation.

Other Forms of Cultural Exchanges

After the founding of the People's Republic of China, the Chinese government made preliminary explorations in foreign cultural exchanges, which helped China open up a new diplomatic situation and enhanced the friendship and understanding between the Chinese people and the other people of the world. But it was not until the launch of Reform and Opening Up Policy in 1978 that China's foreign cultural exchanges truly ushered in the spring of development. China's foreign

影响与机遇

"一带一路"合作范围的不断扩大和合作领域的不断拓展，为其沿线国家及其他地区的国家和组织带来了新的发展机遇，对全球经济的可持续发展产生了重要影响。

首先，"一带一路"催生了新的多边国际发展模式，搭建了跨国合作的优质平台，为推动世界经济的稳定发展奠定了合作基础。

其次，大部分"一带一路"沿线国家为新兴经济体和发展中国家，这不仅为"南南合作"添加了新动力，也推动了全球均衡可持续发展。

最后，"一带一路"共建的过程还推动了各国文化之间的深度交流和传播，为进一步的经贸合作打通了文化壁垒。

其他文化交流形式

新中国成立以后，中国政府在对外文化交流方面做出了初步探索，帮助中国打开了外交的新局面，增进了中国人民与世界其他国家人民之间的友谊和了解。但直到1978年改革开放政策实施以后，中国的对外文化交流才真正迎来了发展的春天。中国的对外文化交流主要包括官方对外文化交流

cultural exchanges mainly include official foreign cultural exchanges and unofficial foreign cultural exchanges.

Official foreign cultural exchanges mainly refer to cultural, artistic and sports exchanges conducted by the government as the main body or main participant. In the early days of the founding of the People's Republic of China, the foreign cultural exchange activities led by the Chinese government mainly consisted of sending cultural, artistic and sports groups to perform, exchange and visit abroad, such as the Peking Opera Troupe's overseas tours, "cultural relics diplomacy" and "ping pong diplomacy". At the same time, China also introduced many Western classical art categories such as ballet, symphony, opera, oil painting, etc., which promoted the prosperity of Chinese culture and art. After the launch of Reform and Opening-Up, China's foreign cultural exchanges became richer in content, more diverse in form, and wider in scope. By the beginning of the 21st century, China had signed cultural cooperation agreements with more than 100 countries in the world, which has led to hundreds of foreign cultural exchange projects. At the same time, with the continuous enhancement of China's economic strength, the influence of Chinese culture in the world has become stronger. China has promoted China's excellent traditional culture and art overseas through platforms such as Confucius Institutes, Chinese language classes, and other forms of overseas Chinese cultural centers. Chinese martial arts, calligraphy, Peking Opera, Tai Chi and other traditional cultural arts have gradually become China's overseas cultural cards, adding a beautiful oriental color to the prosperity of the world

和非官方对外文化交流。

官方对外文化交流主要是指政府作为主体或主要参与方开展的文化、艺术和体育方面的对外交流活动。新中国成立初期，中国政府主导的对外文化交流活动以派遣文化、艺术和体育团体到国外进行演出、交流和访问为主，如京剧艺术团海外巡演、"文物外交"和"乒乓外交"。同时，中国还引进了芭蕾舞、交响乐、歌剧、油画等许多西方古典艺术门类，促进了中国文化和艺术的繁荣。改革开放以后，中国的对外文化交流的内容更加丰富，形式更加多样，领域更加宽广。到21世纪初，中国已经与世界上100多个国家签署了文化合作协定，促成了几百个对外文化交流项目。同时，随着中国经济实力的不断增强，中国文化在国际上的影响力越来越大。中国以孔子学院、汉语课堂和其他形式的海外中国文化中心为平台，将中国优秀的传统文化与艺术推广到了海外。中国的武术、书法、京剧、太极拳及其他传统文化艺术已经逐渐成为中国在海外的文化名片，为世界文化的繁荣增添了一抹美丽的东方色彩。

culture.

China's implementation of foreign cultural exchange activities has not only stayed at the national and governmental level. All kinds of enterprises, social organizations and individuals have also fully exerted their respective strengths, and established reasonable linkage mechanisms and cooperative relations. A new pattern has been formed in which multiple subjects such as the government, social organizations, and enterprises participate together.

First of all, the international cultural exchange activities led by social organizations related to culture are generally weak in ideology and government behavior, and their activities are usually more flexible, and can resonate with both parties through professional exchanges, thus producing good communication effects. Non-governmental organizations such as the China International Culture Exchange Association and the China International Cultural Exchange Center have been committed to enhancing mutual understanding and friendly cooperation between Chinese people and people from other countries since their establishment, and have made positive efforts in spreading Chinese culture and enhancing cultural attraction.

Secondly, foreign cultural exchange activities led by cultural enterprises are generally market-based foreign cultural services and the export of cultural goods. In recent years, the communication activities led by cultural enterprises have become more frequent and have far-reaching influence.

Finally, non-governmental organizations' cultural exchange activities with foreign countries are often carried out by overseas Chinese who live abroad and

中国实施对外文化交流活动不仅仅停留在国家和政府层面，各类企业、社会组织以及个人也充分发挥了各自的力量，建立了合理的联动机制以及合作关系，已经形成了多主体（如政府、社会组织和企业）共同参与的新格局。

首先，与文化相关的社会组织主导的国际文化交流活动，一般意识形态和政府行为较弱，且活动方式通常较为灵活，能够通过专业的交流引起双方的共鸣，从而产生良好的沟通效果。如中国对外文化交流协会、中国国际文化交流中心等非政府组织，自成立以来就一直致力于增进中国人民与世界其他国家人民之间的相互了解以及友好合作，在传播中华文化、增强文化吸引力等方面已经取得了积极的成效。

其次，文化企业主导的对外文化交流活动，一般是以市场为基础的对外文化服务和文化商品出口。近年来，文化企业主导的交流活动愈加频繁，影响深远。

最后，非政府组织的对外文化交流活动往往由旅居海外、心系祖国的华人开展，通过非政府组织的

care for the motherland. They promote the official culture through non-governmental friendly work, such as international photography contests and mutual visits by folk art exchange groups. It can be said that the current non-governmental cultural exchanges with foreign countries have become an important form of global promotion of Chinese culture beyond government guidance and corporate market behavior.

友好工作,如国际摄影大赛、民间艺术交流团互访,以民促官。可以说,当前非政府组织对外文化交流已经成为政府主导和企业市场行为之外的中国文化全球推广的重要形式。

Exercises:

Ⅰ. Questions

1. What does the "Belt" and the "Road" mean in the term the "Belt and Road"?
2. What are the cooperation priorities of the "Belt and Road" Initiative?
3. Can all countries in the world participate in the "Belt and Road" Initiative? Why?

Ⅱ. Group Discussion

Do you know any other important information about the "Belt and Road" Initiative? Share with your classmates.

Suggested Reading:

The Silk Roads was written by Peter Frankopan and published by Zhejiang University Press (2016). It is an all-encompassing epic masterpiece. The author takes the Silk Road as the main line and shows the historical scenery that has been intentionally or unintentionally obscured, ignored, and distorted by historical narratives since modern times. It helps us to understand the complicated interest disputes and thorns on the Silk Road more clearly.

在编写本书的过程中,我们参考、引用和改编了国内外出版的部分相关资料、网络资源,著作权人看到本书后请与我社联系,我社会按照相关法律的规定给予您稿酬。

看配套微课视频
听英语学习音频

主题微课
视频讲解重难点知识，加深印象、巩固所学。

四级微课
视频讲解，直击核心考点，高效备考英语四级。

· **英语学习**
每天一个知识点，实用英语口语轻松学。

· **读书笔记**
记录学习感悟，分享阅读心得。

微信扫码